Wayshowing>Wayfinding

Per Mollerup
Wayshowing>Wayfinding
Basic & Interactive

BIS Publishers
Building Het Sieraad
Postjesweg 1
1057 DT Amsterdam
The Netherlands
T +31 (0)20 515 02 30
F +31 (0)20 515 02 39
bis@bispublishers.nl
www.bispublishers.nl

ISBN 978 90 6369 323 7

Design Per Mollerup

Copyright © 2013 Per Mollerup

All rights reserved. No part of this publication may be reproduced or transmitted in any form or by any means, electronic or mechanical, including photocopy, recording or any information storage and retrieval system, without permission in writing from the copyright owner.

Wayshowing enables wayfinding

Wayshowing>Wayfinding
Introduction, 6

PRINCIPLES

Doing without, 8
  Signage without signs, 9
  Vox populi, 14
Wayfinding, 18
  A problem solving process, 19
  Planning and execution, 21
  Cognitive maps, 24
  Wayfinding strategies, 26
  Track following, 28
  Route following, 30
  Educated seeking, 34
  Inference, 36
  Screening, 38
  Aiming, 40
  Map reading, 42
  Compassing, 44
  Social navigation, 46
  Mixed strategies, 48
  Serendipity, 49
Wayshowing, 50
  Trailblazing, 51
  Environment, 53
  Landmarks, 54
  Toponomy, 56
  Signs, 60
  Maps, 62
  Help desks, 66
  Pre-visit information, 68
  Simplicity vs. redundancy, 70
Practical theory, 72
  A theory of signs, 73
  Messages, 74
  Signification, 75
  Icons, 76
  Indices, 77
  Symbols, 78
  Levels of communication, 80
  Why signs don't work, 82
Sign functions, 86
  Sign categories, 87
  Identification, 90
  Direction, 92
  Description, 94
  Regulation, 96

Sign contents, 98
  Typography, 99
  Pictograms, 106
  Arrows and more, 112
  Guidelines, 117
Sign form, 118
  Colour, 119
  Size, 127
  Format, 128
  Grids, 130
  Grouping, 132
Mise en scène, 134
  Location, 135
  Orientation, 137
  Height, 138
  Mounting, 140
  Lighting, 144
Signs for visually impaired users, 146
  Inclusive vs. exclusive design, 147
  Visual impairments, 149
  Means, 150
Interactive wayshowing, 156
  A digital friend, 157
  WWW, 158
  Kiosks, 159
  Smartphone apps, 160
  QR codes, 164
  AR, Augmented Reality, 165
Planning, 166
  The need for planning, 167
  The planning process, 168
  Branding considerations, 174

PRACTICES

Cases in point, 177

Airport
    Berlin Brandenburg Airport, 178
    Brisbane Airport, 182
    Qantas check-in, 184
    Washington Dulles International Airport, 186

Rail
    JR Tokai Shinkansen, 188
    JR Japan Railways, QR codes, 190
    MTA, New York, 192
    NSB Norwegian State Railways, 194

City
    TriMet Portland Transit Mall, 196
    Trade Fair Stuttgart, 198
    Eureka Parking, Melbourne, 200
    Water Formula, Laboratório Central, Lisbon, 202
    Escaping a tsunami, Santa Barbara, 204

Knowledge
    Vancouver Community Library, 206
    The State Library of New South Wales, Sydney, 208
    Upper Austrian Federal State Library, Linz, 210
    British Library, London, 212
    Osnabrück University of Applied Science, 214

Culture
    Auckland Art Gallery, Toi o Tamaki, 216
    Maritime Museum Rotterdam, 218
    TAP – Théâtre et Auditorium Poitiers, 220
    Royal Botanic Gardens, Kew, 222

Outdoor
    Bikeway, Lisbon, 224
    Melbourne Park, 226
    Falls Creek Alpine Resort, 228

End matter
    Index, 230
    Sources, 234
    Photo credits, 237
    Acknowledgements, 238

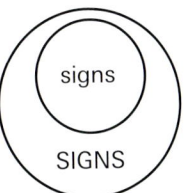

Terminology
In *Wayshowing>Wayfinding (W>W)*, the word 'SIGN' written with upper case letters stands for anything that carries a meaning. The word 'sign' written with lower case letters stands for graphic messages in the environment that help wayfinders to get around.

Heuristics
Throughout the book this symbol marks heuristics, rules of thumbs.

Introduction

Much has happened since the publication of *Wayshowing: A Guide to Environmental Signage* in 2005. The book is long out of print with shamefully high prices on the second-hand market. *Wayshowing>Wayfinding (W>W)* is a revised and expanded version.

Wayshowing coined the term 'wayshowing'. The term has now entered the English language to refer to the professional activity of planning and implementing orientation systems in buildings and outdoor areas. Before *Wayshowing* was published, this professional activity was incorrectly described as 'wayfinding'. Wayshowing and wayfinding relate to each other like writing and reading. Wayshowing precedes and enables wayfinding.

The term 'wayfinding' has its own uses. Wayfinding is what we do when finding our way in unknown quarters. Good wayshowing is user-led, built on how we practice wayfinding. The title, *W>W,* refers to this connection.

The principles in *W>W* have been revised and augmented by a chapter on interactive wayshowing (often referred to in the trade as digital wayfinding).

The presentation of the practices is completely new. This includes 25 examples of wayshowing in action.

W>W has been written to facilitate several reading styles. It can be read from cover to cover, by menu picking, and by using the index to find specific subjects.

Per Mollerup
Melbourne and Copenhagen, 2013

Figure 1 The ultimate helpdesk? Travellers on JR Japan Railways fancy the polite self-service offered by ticket vending machines. If travellers can't find what they are looking for, they push a call button, a little window opens, and a friendly railway officer pops out to assist.

Doing without

Showing the way using signs occupies a large part of this book. This is not because signage is the only wayshowing medium, nor because signage is necessarily the best wayshowing medium. It is because signage is the medium at hand in most practical situations. However, much wayshowing takes place without professional planning and signposting, sometimes without signs, and wayfinders must frequently make do with absolutely unprofessional signs.

Doing without
Signage without signs

User instructions sometimes function as repair design for poorly designed products that do not show how they should be used, or – in severe cases – what they should be used for. Users often feel that the product would have been designed differently if the user instructions had been written concurrently with the product design. So it is with signs in the built environment.

Building signs often announce what the building itself should demonstrate. There can be several reasons for this. One explanation is that architects and other planners rarely design self-explanatory structures. Constructivists, deconstructivists, and many other 'ism' architects consider architecture an expressive art where functional requirements come second. Rather than telling what the building is for or how it should be used, they have other messages in mind. Many architects simply don't care about the 'visual user interface' of their buildings.

A traditional Danish countryside church exemplifies the extent to which a building can explain what should ideally be explained without using signs. When touring the Danish countryside, travellers can generally spot the church from a long distance. The countryside church has a tall belfry. The shape of the church is characteristic and conventional. Most churches look like other churches. The shape of the church makes it easy to recognise from a distance. By the same token, the church also reveals the compass directions. The belfry is traditionally located at the western end of the building. A visitor approaching the church will be in no doubt where to enter. The entrance looks like an entrance. No other part of the façade looks like that. Inside the church, the design tells visitors where to sit, where the priest will be, and where the music will come from. No signs are required to state that visitors should refrain from smoking, eating, or drinking in the church. Without signs, the church manages to tell everyone where it is, what it is, where to enter, where to sit, and how to behave.

2

Figure 2 Danish countryside church. No signs are needed, outdoors or indoors. Intended users know what the church is, how to find it, where to enter, how to use it, and how to behave. Anisse, Denmark.

Signage without signs

In terms of explaining themselves, traditional Danish countryside churches are not unique. Other regions have vernacular buildings with similar visual qualities. Traditional Danish countryside churches, old Dutch windmills, and many other vernacular buildings have generic shapes that reveal their use.

The Danish countryside church and the Dutch windmill function without signs because they meet two requirements. First, the design of churches and windmills follows a tradition. Second, users are familiar with that tradition. There is nothing unknown that signs must explain.

3

Other buildings have shapes that reveal what the buildings are all about, straight away and without tradition. A Los Angeles hotdog stand shaped as a hotdog is a case in point. In *Learning from Las Vegas* Robert Venturi, Denise Scott Brown, and Steven Izenour dubbed this type of allegoric buildings 'ducks' after a duck-shaped building on Long Island.

Robert Venturi, Denise Scott Brown, and Steven Izenour, *Learning from Las Vegas*, MIT Press, Cambridge, Massachusetts, 1972

Most buildings are not as outspoken in their architectural message as the Los Angeles hotdog stand. One reason is that most architects and building owners don't fancy that type of expressive architecture. Another reason is that most buildings change purpose over time. Mies van der Rohe reportedly told his students not to take function too seriously when designing a new building. Eventually, most buildings will be used for a purpose different from the one for which they were originally intended.

Buildings may be characteristic to a degree that allows them to serve as landmarks. Sydney's Opera House is an example. Many high-rise buildings around the world are genuine landmarks. Among these are New York's Empire State Building and the Chrysler Building. The Guggenheim museums in New York and Bilbao, and the Eiffel Tower and the Centre Pompidou in Paris are other renowned architectural landmarks. Landmark buildings are signs in their own right. They show the way to themselves, identify themselves, and facilitate general wayfinding in their area.

Figure 3 Centre Pompidou in Paris, designed by Renzo Piano and Richard Rogers, serves as a landmark because of size and character. A fragment is enough to identify the building.

Figure 4 Tail of the Pup hotdog stand in downtown Los Angeles. The edifice is self-explanatory and makes signage more or less redundant.

Figure 5 Fine produce is its own best advertisement. Greengrocery. Amalfi, Italy.

4
5

Signage without signs

Physical devices of many kinds may act as spatial markers. In the suburbs around Vienna, a Föhrenbusch – pine bush – hanging outside an inn has long meant that the young local wine, Heurigen, is served. Signage without signs has also given name to the generic term 'red light district'.

Throughout the world, shopkeepers exhibit their merchandise as protruding signs in front of their business. Greengrocers, car sellers, and second-hand shops are just a few examples of retailers who consider the product itself to be their best shop sign.

Sometimes, site owners try to get their message across using physical force to ensure that guests and other users do what the site owners want them to do. The philosophy seems to be that confidence is good but enforcement is better. Instead of wasting money and cluttering the visual environment with signs, physical means communicate the desirable or undesired behaviour to ensure or prevent it. Since time immemorial, property owners have blocked entrances with bars, stones, and bollards that walk the talk: they clearly state what people shouldn't do and what will happen if they do. Spikes that damage car tires and barbed wire that damage the clothes and hurt the body are other cases in point.

Sometimes regulation signs come together with robust means of enforcement. This is the case when road owners use signs that urge motorists to reduce their speed while speed bumps ensure that they do so. Motorists who don't slow down feel the bump.

7
8
9

6

Figure 6 Don't climb over this fence. New York.

Figure 7 Don't enter this path with your car. France.

Figure 8 Speed bumps are self-enforcing signs: Please drive slowly. Santa Barbara, USA.

Figure 9 Stop means 'stop'. Santa Barbara, USA.

Figure 10 Don't sit here if you are not a fakir. Window niche outside bank. Knightsbridge, London.

Figure 11 Stay clear of elephant. Elephantine bumbers at the Carlsberg Breweries' Elephant Gate. Copenhagen.

12 W>W

10

11

Doing without
Vox populi

Signs – as a rule – are signs of authority. Those in power generally commission environmental signs. Rulers and owners use signs to inform and regulate society.

However, a rich flora of unofficial, ad hoc signs exists at the side of professionally designed and produced official signs. These unofficial signs are made by citizens who think for one reason or another that official signs fail to meet their needs. Unofficial signs are the visual voice of the people, a graphic *vox populi*.

Unofficial signs serve several different needs, from necessary wayshowing to pure self-expression. Vagabonds communicate by writing and reading signs outside farms. The signs share information about local opportunities and threats. 'Free food' is better than 'food for work', not to mention 'beware of the dog'. Some civil servants in public offices think that their particular department deserves an extra large or conspicuous sign – they make it and mount it.

Unofficial signs are sometimes the result of irritation caused by the lack of other signs or the lack of sufficiently expressive architecture. Letterheads that state 'This is not room 411' or 'Entrance next door' are symptoms of dysfunctional official wayshowing. Venetian shopkeepers make their own 'Al vaporetto' sign when they are tired of explaining hordes of tourists the way to the ferry to San Marco. According to Nobel Laureate Herbert Simon, design is about devising actions aimed at changing present situations into preferred situations.

Unofficial, do-it-yourself signs are normally the symptoms of unsuccessful planning. Sometimes, however, amateur signs are more credible than professional signs. This is the case when farmers advertise eggs and produce by the roadside. Drivers read hapless graphics as evidence of good-natured innocence.

Figure 12 Unprofessional graphics are sometimes read as circumstantial evidence of commercial innocence. Farmer's roadside advertising. Melby, Denmark.

For obvious reasons, travellers and patients do not grant airlines and hospitals the same freedom of graphic expression as they grant chicken and potato farmers. An 'out of order' sign in the cabin of a commercial aircraft written with a speedmarker will inevitably generate a negative image. Is this really a safe flight?

Some of the world's first signs were probably a kind of graffiti. These trailblazers of visual wayshowing had little resemblance to the graphic weeds that are known as graffiti today. As a rule, contemporary graffiti have no practical purpose beyond that of announcing the existence and egotism of the writers.

Vox populi

Figure 13-16 Visitors to the Oodnadatta Track outback in South Australia, 200 km North East of Coober Pedy, Australia's dryest, hottest town, enjoy truly vernacular wayshowing. The signage was designed, executed, and paid for by the late Adam Plate, owner of Pink Roadhouse Oodnadatta. Adam Plate's signposting covers an area of several hundred square kilometres not found worthy of public signage. The sign content is not limited to names, distances, and directions, but includes all kinds of useful local information. Adam Plate also published mudmaps, musts for travellers in the area. www.pinkroadhouse.com.au

Wayfinding

Good wayshowing design is user-led. It builds on a deep understanding of how we find our way in built or natural environments. This chapter describes wayfinding as a problem solving process and presents the strategies we all use when navigating in terra incognita – unknown land. Most people don't know that they use these strategies. Nevertheless, successful wayshowing depends upon understanding, externalising, and supporting these strategies.

Wayfinding
A problem solving process

Wayfinding is a problem solving process. The basic problem is to find a way from one location to another. The process includes seeking information – searching for an appropriate route, deciding which route to take, and moving along that route. This three-step process is iterative; wayfinders repeat the process until they reach their destination. Search and decision occur off-route as planning before departure and on-route when navigating after departure.

Seeking information means looking for and reading external information and combining it with internal information. External off-route information includes all kinds of advance information given by maps and verbal descriptions. External on-route information covers all cues given by the environment itself, as well as by signs and other kinds of wayshowing aids. Internal information is the traveller's relevant knowledge including his cognitive map, the mental representation of the area.

Deciding covers choosing among identified possible routes. The traveller chooses a route – when there is a choice – by evaluating and comparing the attributes of possible routes. Attributes may include such factors as familiarity, distance, expected traffic, safety, scenic beauty, ease of access, ease of navigation, economy (road tolls, ferry tickets, and other costs) and schedules, if public transport is involved.

**The three-step iterative wayfinding process:
Search, Decision, Motion**

Off-route **Search**
　　　　Initial planning
　　　　Decision
On-route **Motion**
　　　　Search
　　　　Planning
　　　　Navigation
　　　　Decision
　　　　Motion

17

Figure 17 On-route information includes all kinds of signs, official or not. Amsterdam.

A problem solving process

Moving is an integral part of wayshowing. Sitting in a lounge chair at home while finding a route on an automobile map is planning. The human-environment confrontation where the traveller reads the environmental 'user interface' to make decisions while moving is the core business of wayfinding. It is the moment of truth when the traveller's wayfinding capacities join forces with the environment's wayshowing features.

Getting from here to there, from A to B, is the most basic wayshowing problem. It is only one of many:

– Where am I?
– Getting from A to B (from here to there)
– Getting from B back to A (homing)
– Getting from B to C
– Getting from C back to A
– How long will it take?
– What will I see on the road?
– What is out there?
– Where do I find hospitals, shops, etc.?

In fact, some of these questions don't ask for wayshowing in the strict sense of the concept. They involve placeshowing. Placeshowing often precedes wayshowing. A traveller doesn't ask the way to something, that he doesn't know exists. Public transportation fares and schedules may also influence the wayfinding process.

18

Figure 18 Position: Tsing Yi. Destination: Hong Kong. Hong Kong Metro.

Wayfinding
Planning and execution

All journeys are planned, more or less formally, in a more or less detailed manner. Some planning takes place before departure and plans may be adjusted and completed on-route.

Before starting a journey, the traveller thinks ahead, making some decisions. How conscious, careful, and detailed this initial planning is, depends on several factors. The distance to be travelled and the traveller's previous knowledge of possible routes are particularly important factors. Going to the newsstand to buy a newspaper will not call for more planning than deciding to do what one has often done before. The distance is short and knowledge is extensive. Going for the first time from a small town in Europe to a skiing resort in the Rocky Mountains of the United States typically calls for more initial planning. Which airlines fly from and to which airport gateways? What are the schedules and fares? How does one get from the origin to the European airport and from the North American airport to the final destination in the Rockies? Long distances and unfamiliar journeys tend to demand more initial planning than short distances and familiar journeys.

Initial planning is based on the traveller's prior knowledge, perhaps assisted by such off-route information sources as maps, guides, and timetables. Prior knowledge may reduce initial planning for two reasons. First, if the traveller's knowledge is limited and he cannot easily get more information, he may start the journey with a minimum of initial planning. Second, a traveller with thorough knowledge of the route to be travelled may minimise initial planning, confident that he can compensate with on-route search.

On-route planning and decisions may benefit from information about the environment that was not available for initial planning. On-route planning and decisions can also take needs and wants into consideration that did not exist before departure.

Planning and execution

The traveller decides how carefully to plan a journey – or part of a journey. Security is weighed against planning costs. Most of us tend to prefer some planning for long journeys and almost no planning for short journeys. Going long distances without planning may involve large risks. Extensive planning for small trips may not justify the time that planning requires. The choice between planning and finding is a question of personal preference. Some travellers prefer safety. Others seem to reason: I don't plan, I find.

For long journeys, travellers typically divide the total route into a sequence of sections. Some of these sections may be further divided into practical sections of comprehensible size. A practical section of comprehensible size is a section that the traveller considers a planning unit. No further detailed planning is wanted, needed, or possible.

Practical sections may include wayfinding problems that cannot be planned for at all, but only solved as the traveller proceeds: solvitur ambulando. Finding the right departure gate in an airport is one example of this type of wayfinding problem. Solving such problems requires information given on location, typically by the environment and its signs.

Decisions concerning one or more sections ahead are planning decisions. Decisions concerning immediate parts of practical sections are execution decisions. To decide to go from Copenhagen to Helsinki is a planning decision. To decide to take the escalator from the check-in area to the departure hall in Copenhagen Airport is an execution decision. Planning decisions may be taken before departure or on-route. Travellers typically base planning decisions on off-location information. Travellers usually make execution decisions in direct contact with the environment.

The wayfinding process

Planning
1 Decision to move
2 Seeking information – Search
3 Checking internal information
4 Checking external information
5 Computing alternative routes
6 Selecting eligible routes
7 Choosing criteria
8 Evaluating eligible routes
9 Choosing route – Decision
> **Mental solution** = Plan

Execution
10 Move / Search / Decide / Move
> **Physical solution** = Journey completed

Figure 19 The environment may be more or less helpful to the wayfinder seeking on-route information. Gamla Stan, Stockholm.

Wayfinding
Cognitive maps

A traveller's spatial knowledge about a certain area is sometimes referred to as a cognitive map, mental map, or mental model. This is his mental representation of an environment. The cognitive map includes the traveller's internal information about an area, its features and objects, and their spatial relations.

In *The Image of the City,* Kevin Lynch suggests that we remember a city by five components: paths, landmarks, nodes, edges, and districts. These features together with others, such as general character, populate cognitive maps.

Contrary to printed maps, cognitive maps are not static. Information is added to a cognitive map whenever a traveller takes in information about the environment from off-location sources or directly from the environment. Off-location sources include surveys from external maps along with all kinds of verbal and pictorial descriptions. Travellers may acquire information from the environment intentionally by surveying the environment from an elevated position or other kinds of inspection. Aquiring information may also take place unintentionally by passing through a building, townscape, or landscape.

The isolated experience of following a route is generally remembered as a linear experience mentally pictured as a one-dimensional strip-map. When expanded by the experience of following more routes that cross each other, this supposedly builds networks – mental configurations similar to two-dimensional planar maps.

Cognitive maps can become more precise and more comprehensive as more information is absorbed. Conversely, cognitive maps can also become less precise and less comprehensive as time goes by and travellers forget what they once remembered. Cognitive maps also become less precise if they are not updated when the environment changes. Travellers share a common experience when they find that airports, hospitals, and fairgrounds change from time to time and discover that facilities have moved since last visit.

Kevin Lynch
The Image of the City
MIT Press, Cambridge, Massachusetts, 1960

Experts on cognitive maps debate whether information obtained by following routes or information obtained by surveying makes the greater contribution to cognitive maps.

Figure 20 'View of the World from 9th Avenue', 1975. Saul Steinberg's iconic conception of New Yorkers' cognitive map of the world west of 9th Avenue.

Wayfinding
Wayfinding strategies

Travellers choose from an array of wayfinding strategies to execute sections of their journey. Here we define a wayfinding strategy as a rational principle for search, decision, and motion. This definition includes intelligent seeking, but excludes random seeking. Travellers typically practice random seeking when they have lost their way and don't have the faintest idea where they are. They try to find their way without logical reasoning.

Travellers choose among nine wayfinding strategies. The strategy or combination of strategies chosen in any specific situation depends on the traveller's disposition and prior knowledge. It also depends on the information sources at hand, including information offered by the environment through which a way must be found. Travellers typically don't know that they know these strategies.

To some degree, all nine strategies build on reading the environment. The nine strategies are primarily aimed at the built environment. They depend in varying degrees on signage and other wayshowing aids.

Some strategies involve pure rule-following. The traveller simply obeys directions. Other strategies depend on sense-making, a deeper understanding of the problem. Sense-making demands intellectual effort while giving the traveller the freedom to choose preferred ways.

To some degree, modern GPS technology and smartphone maps and apps make wayfinding strategies redundant. However, not all travellers are equipped with – or want to use – these devices. Also, not all areas, especially not indoor areas, which tend to be larger and larger, are covered by GPS maps. In such cases, GPS brings the traveller close to the destination where wayfinding strategies take over.

Nine wayfinding strategies

1 **Track following**
Following signs, lines, or other tracks
2 **Route following**
Following a plan
3 **Educated seeking**
Using prior knowledge
4 **Inference**
Concluding from sequential designations
5 **Screening**
Systematic searching
6 **Aiming**
Visual targeting
7 **Map reading**
Using portable and you-are-here maps
8 **Compassing**
Using compass directions
9 **Social navigation**
Learning from others

Figure 21-22 Wayfinders benefit from all kinds of visual clues.

Figure 21 Seattle.

Figure 22 Tallinn, Estonia

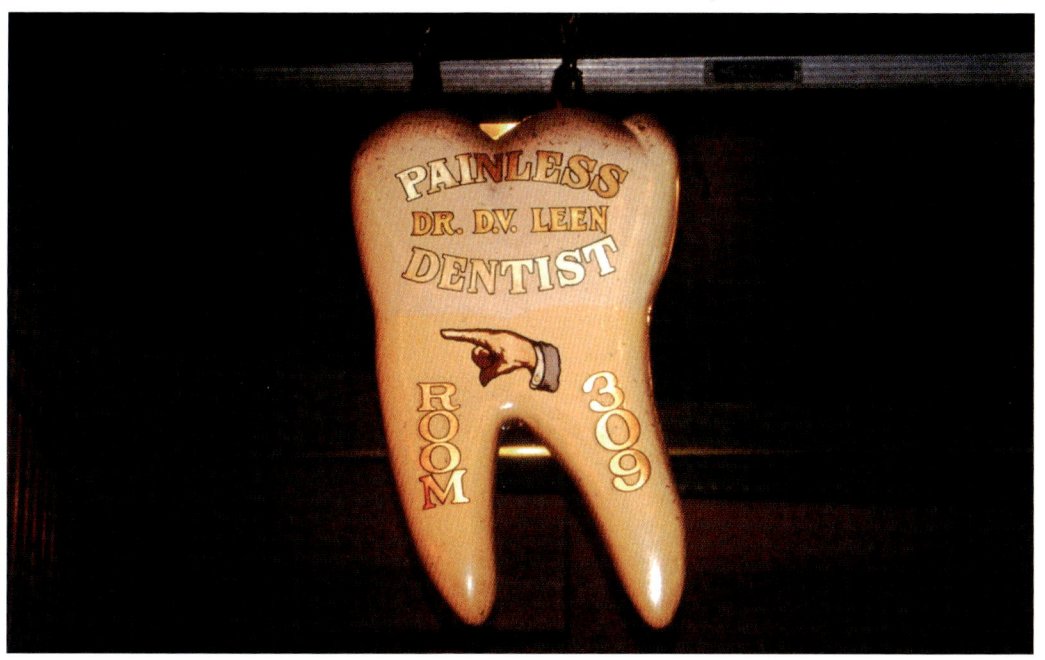

21
22

Wayfinding
Strategy 1: Track following

Ariadne, daughter of King Minos of Crete, created the flagship case of track following when she gave Theseus of Athens a ball of string to enable his escape from the labyrinth after killing the Minotaur.

Next to direct aiming, track following is the most basic wayfinding strategy. Practitioners of this strategy follow a track by using one or more sensory capacities. Humans will follow visual and occasionally tactile and aural tracks. Detectives in novels stereotypically follow visual tracks. Animals often follow olfactory tracks when screening and locating their prey or finding their way back to their point of origin.

Track following takes place whenever we rely on directional signs on the road, or in large buildings. Sometimes, track following is just one of several possible wayfinding strategies. Sometimes it is the only available strategy. The latter is the case when we find ourselves in a large London underground station. We have changed direction so many times that we don't have the faintest idea how we are oriented or situated in the vast and complex subterranean environment. Even the bravest wayfinders must resign themselves to track following and reading directional signs.

Road detours are well-known obstructions to drivers. Roadwork relegates drivers to an alternate route marked by more or less haphazard ad hoc signs. If a driver misses even one of these wayshowing aids, he may have great difficulty getting back 'on the right track'.

Sometimes, a path is itself a track to follow, a psychological tunnel. This is the case in many museums where visitors are supposed to pass several rooms before reaching the exit. It is also the case in such large shopping environments as IKEA stores. In nature, scenic walking and driving routes are sometimes marked by special signage. Riding paths typically show the route by their sheer existence.

For people with normal visual and cognitive abilities, coloured lines in the floor can be useful tracks in hospitals.

Hänsel – one of the two protagonists in Grimm's fairy tale *Hänsel und Gretel* – left a path of breadcrumbs to find their way back when brother and sister walked into the dark woods. Today, website designers include metaphorical breadcrumb trails in their design to help visitors monitor their way around the website.

Figure 23 Track following is the smartest wayfinding strategy in many situations. In some situations, such as road detours, track following is the only way to get back 'on the right track'. Helsinge, Denmark.

Figure 24 The ultimate track following observed in the streets of old Vienna where groups of tourists cling to the guide's blue rope. A mobile version of Ariadne's thread?

23
24

Create psychological tunnels.
Coordinate on-route signs with maps.

Wayfinding
Strategy 2: Route following

We practice route following whenever we follow the directions of a local inhabitant or another expert, or consult a written source about the way to something and follow route instructions. Route following is rule-following. It demands careful perception more than careful thinking. To follow a route instruction is to follow a spatial user instruction. Like other user instructions, route instructions vary in quality. The proverbial 'You can't miss it, Sir', is no guarantee.

The difference between track following and route following is the location of necessary information. In track following, we find the information on the road while travelling. We find it where we need it on-route. In route following, we get information off-route before we start and store it internally in the mind or externally on a piece of paper to be consulted on-route. Track following can be likened to software in a computer that gives on-screen instructions while an activity is in progress. Route following is comparable to assembling a piece of knockdown furniture while following a printed user instruction.

Off-route information used for route following is a kind of recipe that says, first do this, then do that. The instruction can be verbal or pictorial. A verbal instruction can be oral or written. A pictorial instruction can be a route map or a series of pictures describing the route.

Wayfinding strategies can be mixed and used in different combinations. Route following and track following can support each other. We read the guidebook instructions before departure, we follow the suggested route, and use road signs to monitor our movements.

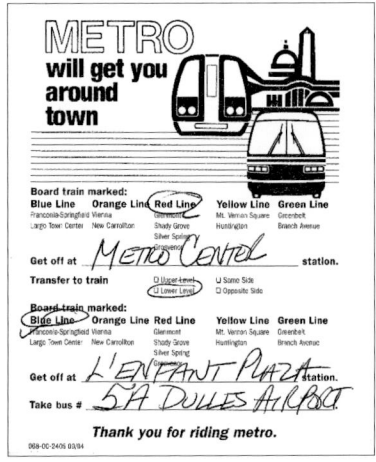

25

Figure 25 Travellers who ask for help at Washington DC Metro stations get a smile and a note with detailed route description such as: Board train marked Red Line. Get off at Metro Center. Transfer to train Lower level. Board train marked Blue Line. Get off at L'Enfant Plaza. Take bus # 5A Dulles Airport.

Figure 26 *No Way Through* published by the British Automobile Association describes walking route proposals in three ways: verbally, by map, and by pictures from the route.

PANORAMIC VIEWPOINT ON THE NORTH DOWNS

Box Hill

South-east England
Walk 39
3½ or 4½ miles

THIS WALK EXPLORES ONE OF THE LESSER-KNOWN ROUTES TO ONE OF the most spectacular viewpoints on the North Downs. A favourite picnic place as long ago as Charles II's reign, Box Hill offers a peaceful beauty unchanged by the passing of time. There are many quiet tracks over the downs and across the wooded slopes; but the descent beyond Point 11 is very steep, and slippery after wet weather.

CAR PARK Picnic area at the foot of Box Hill, near Burford Bridge Hotel on the A24 Leatherhead-Dorking road.

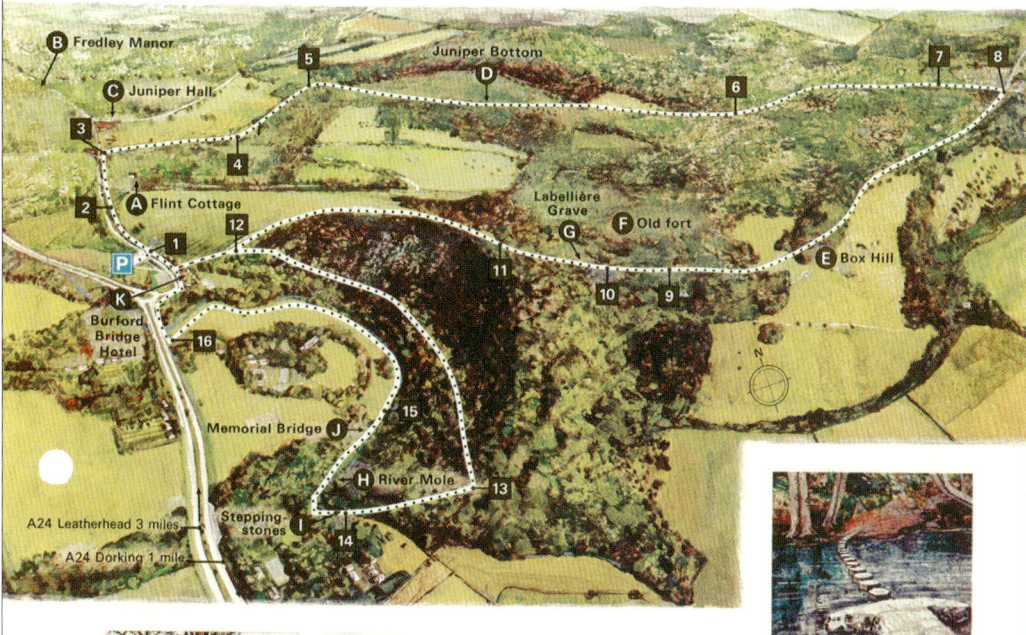

1 Cross road and turn left on path parallel with road

2 Continue ahead on main road past St Jude Lodge

3 At top of rise, take drive on right opposite steps on left

4 Pass Little Pinehurst; keep left at forks, and follow fence to join crossing track at bottom

5 Turn right and walk up valley for nearly a mile

6 Straight on up hill through trees, ignoring crossing tracks

7 At caravan site, follow boundary hedge and fork right along path to road

8 At road, turn right along roadside path to viewpoint

9 About 150 yds beyond viewpoint, at bend by car park exit notice, take path to left, keeping fence on left

10 At cross path on edge of hill, bear right and pass Labellière Grave on to chalk track along ridge

11 Where path forks, branch left down hill alongside trees towards hotel

12 Just before wire fence near foot of hill, turn left along narrow path for nearly ½ mile. Take great care of steep drops. [To shorten walk, continue down hill and across road to car park]

13 Fork right down steps. At foot of steps bear right down hill and continue straight ahead to river

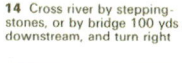

14 Cross river by stepping-stones, or by bridge 100 yds downstream, and turn right

15 Over stile and follow riverside path

16 At road turn right, back to car park

Route following

Homing – returning to the point of origin – involves a special kind of problem solved primarily by route following. The 'route description' is the information gathered on the way out. It is stored as part of a cognitive map, possibly reinforced by notes taken on the way out. A number of problems are associated with homing:

First, we experience a route differently depending on the direction in which we move. What we see when moving in one direction may be quite different from what we see when moving in the opposite direction.

Second, a certain route may objectively be more complicated in one direction than in the other. If a number of road forks are oriented in the same way, the route may appear simple driving in one direction and complicated driving in the other direction.

Third, a number of planned or incidental obstructions may hinder homing along exactly the same route back as used on the way out. Unidirectional streets, separated entrances and exits, one-way doors, and roads blocked by accidents can make homing difficult.

These kinds of tribulations may worsen if outbound travel takes place in daylight while homing takes place after dark. A familiar homing situation occurs when a traveller accompanied by a local guide on the way out in daylight didn't pay attention to the route before trying to find the way back alone after dark.

Design for transparency.
Create landmarks.
Make on-route identification signs.

When you come to a fork in the road, take it.
Yogi Berra

How to reach the West Indies from Europe? Sail south till the butter melts, then due west.
Early navigator's maxim

Figure 27 Children who mistakenly leave the Copenhagen Zoo through this one-way door cannot easily find the way back to their parents. Homing is obstructed.

Wayfinding
Strategy 3: Educated seeking

Educated seeking is a spatial variety of educated guessing. Unlike random seeking, it is an intelligent approach for wayfinding. Educated seeking works by syllogism, the type of logical method originally described by Aristotle:

Major premise	All men are mortal.
Minor premise	Socrates is a man.
Conclusion	Therefore, Socrates is mortal.

If A and B, then C. The crux of the matter is the validity of the premises.

Educated seeking takes place, for example, when a customer wants to buy a litre of milk in a supermarket where he has never been before. He immediately proceeds to the farthest end of the market. He remembers that most supermarkets store necessary daily basics in the most remote part of the sales area – to expose customers to as many temptations as possible on their way to and from the essentials, he thinks*. Our customer's educated guess is that this supermarket organises its stock in the same way that most supermarkets do.

This example of educated seeking can be phrased as a syllogism:

Major premise	Most supermarkets store milk in the farthest end of the shop.
Minor premise	This is a supermarket.
Conclusion	The milk in this supermarket is probably stored in the farthest end of the shop.

The vague quality of the major premise: 'most supermarkets' is reflected in the vague conclusion: 'probably'. This is a common feature of educated seeking.

> Truly intelligent behaviour calls for the ability to use information acquired in one situation to solve problems in another.
> Arno Penzias, Nobel Laureate

> **Intelligence is the art of good guesswork.**
> H.B. Barlow

*The truth is that supermarkets often store dairy products at the back wall to enable stocking the racks with heavy dairy products from behind.

Figure 28 Most supermarkets store milk and other dairy products in the farthest end of the shop. Educated seekers know that and take advantage. Melbourne.

34 W>W

Educated seeking is a common form of wayfinding. We don't look for a gas station on a narrow street in a sleepy residential area. We look on a broad heavily trafficked road. We look for speciality shops in the town centre and we seek marine supplies near the harbour. In the hospital, we look for the newsstand in the main lobby. We expect to find airport check-in counters near the landside entrance. Educated seeking works by sense-making.

Use common patterns when planning environments for wayfinding.

Wayfinding
Strategy 4: Inference

Inference as a wayfinding strategy means using the structural qualities of street numbers, house numbers, entrance letters, and other ordinal information given on signs to infer the larger structure of the environment.

By seeing 57th and 58th Street, a traveller in Manhattan infers by extrapolation the way to 59th Street. Another traveller who has passed 57th and 58th Street and sees 60th Street understands by interpolation that he has passed 59th Street without noticing it. Numbered motor road exits function in the same way and so do house numbers in most cities in the western world. Stadium gates, platform sections, and lifeboat stations marked A, B, C, etc. also function this way. The organising principle can be any string of entities used in a generally accepted sequence. In a museum, years, or archaeological periods could be organising principles.

Inference depends heavily on the numerical and alphabetical toponomy – naming of places – including an apparent structural analogy between the signifier and the signified. The stadium gates marked A-H must follow each other as the letters in the alphabet do.

The inference strategy also depends on a certain element of environmental business-as-usual. Travellers who see that all houses on one side of the street are even will easily jump to the conclusion that house numbers on the other side of the street are odd and rise in the same direction. In some quarters that may not be true.

Inference is a variety of educated seeking. It works by sense-making.

Apply sequentially ordered designations.
Follow common cultural patterns.
Create comprehensible structures.

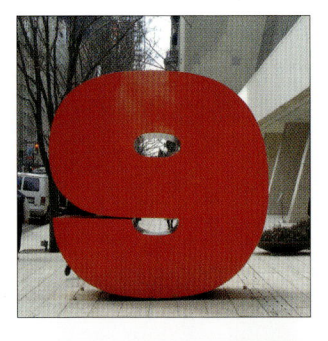

29
30
31

Figure 29 The iconic house number on New York's 57th Street that became a landmark. Design Chermayeff & Geismar.

Figure 30 The coffee shop neighbouring New York's famous '9' pays its respect by its Felliniesque '8½'.

Figure 31 Seattle house owners use half numbers to avoid breaking the logic of sequential house numbers.

32

33, 34

Figure 32 By inference, spectators at Parken Stadium in Copenhagen can read signs they can't see.

Figure 33-34 In one street in Riga, the problem of identifying two houses sharing one number is solved in two different ways. Which one is better?

W>W 37

Wayfinding
Strategy 5: Screening

The screening strategy involves searching an area systematically for something specific, either a destination or a clue. Unlike educated seeking, screening will lead to a solution if there is one, or reveal that there is no solution. On the other hand, screening may be quite pedestrian, involving a great deal of activity where educated seeking may lead directly to the target. If a milk buyer screens the supermarket starting at the entrance and the milk is in the most remote part of the sales area, he will reach his goal only after he has inspected almost every shelf in the supermarket. Here, as elsewhere good thinking may replace walking.

Depending on the kind of decision process used, screening may be limited or total. Travellers looking for a specific target or wanting to satisfice*, choose limited screening. Travellers who want to optimise choose total screening.

Decision type	Screening type
– targeting	– limited
– satisficing	– limited
– optimising	– total

*Satisfice, a portmanteau word based on the words 'satisfy' and 'suffice', is a decision-making strategy suggested by Herbert Simon. Satisficing implies that good enough is enough, contrary to optimising: when only the best will do.

– A tourist screening a seaside resort in search of a specific hotel will stop screening when he finds his hotel. Decision type: targeting; screening type: limited.

– A car driver running out of gas who screens an area for an open gas station will stop screening when he finds the first open gas station. Decision type: satisficing; screening type: limited.

– A stroller who wants an espresso at a sidewalk café screens the total serving area to find the sunny position with the best isovist – view from a specific point. Decision type: optimising; screening type: total.

Design for transparency.
Organise systematically.
Make area accessible.

Figure 35 Guests with a booking at Hotel Parsifal, Ravello, Italy, stop screening when they see this entrance.

Figure 36 Car drivers out of gas stop screening when they see an open station, no matter what brand.

Figure 37 Sidewalk café guests make a total screening to find the best vacant table.

35
36
37

Wayfinding
Strategy 6: Aiming

Aiming – the simplest wayfinding strategy – means moving in the direction of a perceptible target. That target will typically be a vertical outlier. Direct aiming means the target itself is immediately perceptible. Indirect aiming means that the target is not perceptible, but something near to it is.

A visitor to Paris who wants to go to the Eiffel Tower will just look and walk in that direction. This is direct aiming. A visitor who wants to go to a place near the Eiffel Tower will walk in direction of the tower, only focussing on details when he gets close to the tower. This is indirect aiming.

While direct aiming is a pure rule-following strategy, indirect aiming includes an element of sense-making.

Create landmarks and transparency.

Figure 38-39 Aiming extraordinaire. From a certain spot at the Town Hall Square in Tallinn, Estonia, seven church spires can be seen. A friendly houseowner has cut a piece of his roof to enable the view of the seventh spire – of the Holy Ghost Church.

Figure 40 The Eureka Tower in Melbourne is a 297m high vertical outlier. Can be seen from most parts of the central metropolitan area.

Wayfinding
Strategy 7: Map reading

Map reading as a wayfinding strategy involves portable maps and stationary maps.

Reading a portable map allows the wayfinder to get a large-scale overview of the territory to be travelled. Compared with a good view from a helicopter or a high tower, the map offers at least three advantages. First, the map is portable. Second, the map – in principle – offers only relevant information. Irrelevant information is left out. Third, the map reveals the names of relevant wayfinding phenomena.

Efficient map reading implies that the wayfinder knows where he is and where he wants to go. The task is to find one or more eligible routes and choose the preferred route from here to there. The map-reader looks for correspondence between the map and the world around him.

Using a map that describes a certain territory involves sense-making. Using a map that just shows one route involves rule-following – route following according to our classification.

Stationary maps in the environment are typically so-called you-are-here maps *(see page 62)*, generally abbreviated as y-a-h maps. They have two advantages and one disadvantage compared with portable maps. The first advantage is that y-a-h maps make it unnecessary for the traveller to carry a portable map. The second advantage is that y-a-h maps are marked to demonstrate the exact location of the traveller. The disadvantage is that the user must remember the information given by the y-a-h map when he moves on. He cannot take it with him.

Coordinate names on maps and signs.
Create alignment between map and reality.

Figure 41 Legible London. Design AIG Applied Information Group.

Figure 42 You-are-here map of ATC Advanced Technologies Centre, Swinburne University of Technology. Melbourne.

41

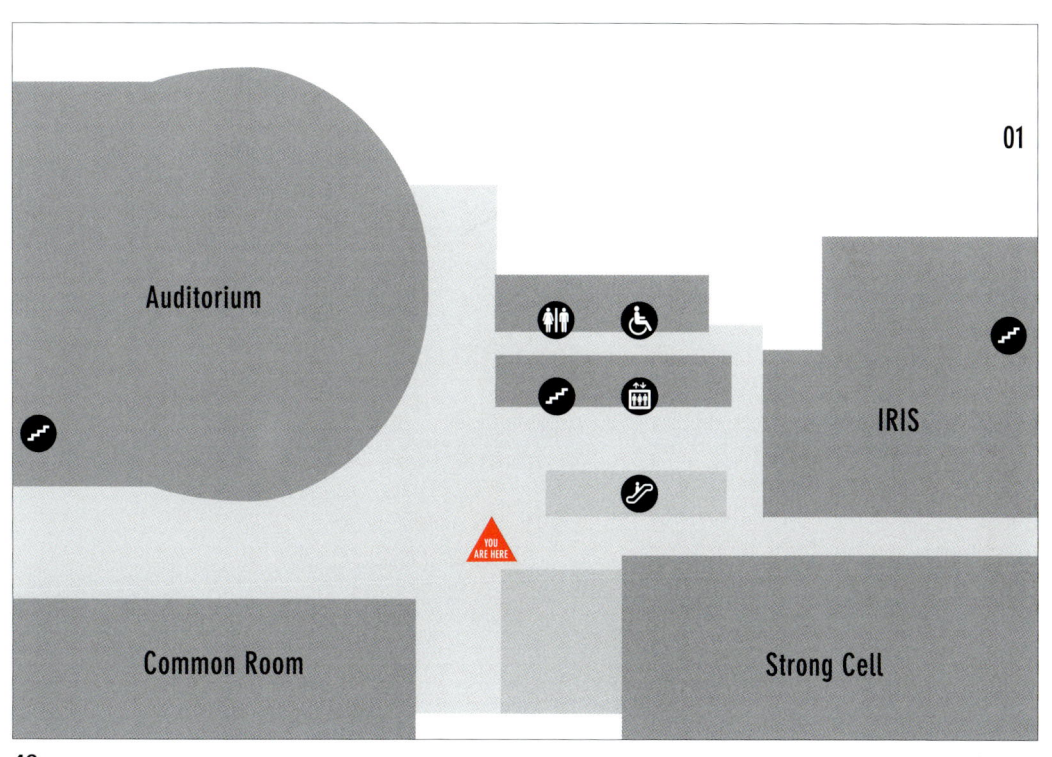

42

Wayfinding
Strategy 8: Compassing

Using compass directions for wayfinding – with or without a compass – can be an excellent strategy in open landscapes as well as in built environments. Two conditions must be met for this strategy to be useful. First, the wayfinder must have an idea of the relative position of his present location and his destination. Second, the wayfinder must be able to determine compass directions, either by use of a compass or by reading one or more clues in the environment.

The wayfinder's cognitive map will often include a rough idea of compass directions. In Paris, all residents and many visitors know that the river Seine runs east-west. In Chicago, the lakeshore runs roughly north-south. Manhattan is known for its east-west streets and north-south avenues. When the sun is shining, this fact – combined with local time – reveals the orientation. So do other manmade and natural phenomena. In western Denmark, solitary trees lean towards the east because of the prevailing westerly winds. In the northern hemisphere, moss grows on the northern shadow-side of stones and trees. Finally, place and building names such as West Wing, Southgate, and North Tower also indicate compass directions.

Wayfinding by compassing is most often used in concert with other strategies, sometimes as a sensible way to monitor route following.

Include compass directions in place names.

Figure 43-44 Some buildings include compass directions in their names and signage. La Bibliotèque Nationale de France, Paris.

43
44

Wayfinding
Strategy 9: Social navigation

Social navigation means that the wayfinder navigates by learning from other people's present or past actions. The wayfinder reads social signifiers. Consider a traveller who has lost his way in Venice and finds himself on a small campo (Venetian for square), from which seven alleys lead away. A time-honoured practice in the lagoon city is to learn from other people. If all people leaving the campo use one of two alleys, and the traveller came in by one, then he should leave by the other. The other five alleys probably lead nowhere. Crowdsourcing says so.

In the Venetian example, the wayfinder learns from other people's present actions. Sometimes other people's previous actions may show the way. A small path in the forest tells us that other people have walked here. The path silently announces this is the way. The environment is historically enriched. In fact, all roads and streets provide evidence of other people's previous actions. In some cases, the difference between track following and social navigation is marginal.

Design for transparency.

Figure 45 Venetian campo. Follow the crowd. Illustration from Ebbe Sadolin, *Vandringer i Venedig* (Walking in Venice).

Figure 46 Queue spotting is a time-honoured wayfinding discipline. From a distance, visitors see where the action is. Funicular. Bergen, Norway.

45

46

W>W 47

Wayfinding
Mixed strategies

In practice, travellers use a mix of wayfinding strategies. A traveller asks a passer-by for the way to an antique market and practices route following. At the antique market, he consults a directory, and makes his way to the fourth floor by track following. A staircase is a track. On the fourth floor, he screens the stalls to find the section for vintage fountain pens.

The traveller using mixed strategies will often start by using a strategy based on off-route information and continue using a strategy based on on-route information.

Make destinations recognisable by variety, hierarchy, relative position, and identification signs.

47

Figure 47 First time visitors to the Atletion sports compound in Aarhus, Denmark, will probably find their way by route following and track following. Once there, they will find their hall, court or course, track or field, and their particular seat, or perhaps the Break Café, by a combination of map reading, track following, and aiming. Design Mollerup Designlab.

Wayfinding
Serendipity

Is finding the way the only happy solution to a wayfinding problem? Yes and no. We search to find, but sometimes the journey is as important, or more important, than the goal. It all depends on the circumstances.

If we have had an accident and must go to the hospital emergency ward, we want to find the location as soon as possible. The same is true, if we must catch a flight, attend an opera performance, or get to an important job interview. It is different if we are on holiday and we wish to go for a stroll in Venice. We may possibly want to end at Caffè Florian on St. Mark's Square, but a little waylosing on the way doesn't hurt. In fact, waylosing is a cherished part of the Venetian experience. Real labyrinths and mazes have no other purposes than letting users enjoy the pleasure of getting lost.

When losing our way, we see things we otherwise wouldn't have seen. These unsolicited experiences are sometimes worth as much or more than the originally intended targets. Serendipity, good luck in making unexpected and fortunate discoveries, finding an America when looking for an India, should not be neglected.

Even then, the purpose of *W>W* is to help designers helping wayfarers to find their destinations with the desired efficiency.

> **No matter what you set for as you leave the house here, you are bound to get lost in these long coiling lanes and passageways that beguile to see them through, to follow them to their elusive end, which usually hits water, so you can't even call it a cul-de-sac. On the map this city looks like two grilled fish sharing a plate, or perhaps like two overlapping lobster claws (Pasternak compared it to a swollen croissant); but it has no north, south, east, or west; the only direction it has is sideways. It surrounds you like frozen seaweed, and the more you dart and dash about to get your bearings, the more you get lost.**
> Joseph Brodsky in *Watermark*

Figure 48 Waylosing, being trapped in dead ends, is a cherished part of the Venetian experience.

Wayshowing

Wayshowing includes all the activities and implements that make a location navigable: identifiable, understandable, memorable, and accessible. It follows that wayshowing aids may be implicit parts of the location as well as explicit features added with wayshowing as their only function. Politicians, town planners, architects, and designers all contribute to making a location navigable for the wayfinder. This chapter presents the major wayshowing parameters.

Wayshowing
Trailblazing

Since time immemorial, humans have practiced wayshowing, when they helped other humans to find the way to food and friends by leaving clues in the environment. A trailblazer was a person who literally left marks on trees.

Wayshowing and wayfinding relate to each other as do writing and reading, teaching and learning, or cooking and eating. One activity deals with sending, the other with receiving. The purpose of wayshowing is to facilitate wayfinding.

Wayshowing can facilitate the wayfinding strategies presented in the previous chapter through informative wayshowing provisions. The heuristics in this book highlight those provisions.

A sufficient number of relevant signs can solve most wayfinding problems. However, cost and respect for the environment limit the acceptable number of signs. The preferred solution will always be a readable environment supported by the least number of signs that are necessary, but not fewer.

In all wayfinding strategies, destinations must be recognisable. Reaching a destination without recognising it – being there without knowing it – is bad luck.

Good wayshowing starts with planning, whether planning a landscape, a town, a quarter, or a large building. Wayfinding-friendly environments include elements of repetition as well as variation. Repetition facilitates global understanding by likeness while variation facilitates local wayfinding by difference. Too much likeness and too much variation both impede wayfinding. Planning requires a balance between repetitive systems and variation. Neither a town with all houses completely alike nor a town with all houses completely different will facilitate wayfinding. We want a recognisable system with some variation. An effective maze is characterised by the lack of both elements.

Trailblazing

Hierarchical environments help the users of most wayfinding strategies. Designed difference is one way of showing hierarchy. A broad street, a large house, and a large sign all signify importance by their sheer size. The orientation of a sign may also indicate its relative importance. Signs positioned perpendicular to the direction of the traffic are seen as more important than signs shown sideways along the road. Lighted streets and signs indicate more importance than unlighted streets and signs.

As already noted, signs are not the only wayshowing aids, however visible they may be. In fact, signs should be used as the wayshowing means of last resort. The following sections of this book present the battery of wayshowing aids.

Wayshowing
Environment

Self-explanatory environments are preferable to all other wayshowing implements.

When we buy a new power tool, we prefer one that immediately tells us how to use it. This is the same with locations. The second best solution is labels with user instructions printed on the tool. The third best solution involves separate user instructions. In wayshowing terms, these three solutions are a self-explanatory environment, an environment that is not self-explanatory, but that is explained with signs, and an environment that is not self-explanatory and has no signs, but can be explained with portable maps.

Business-as-usual plays a central role for self-explanatory tools and environments. A door that looks like a door and an entrance that looks like an entrance need no signs saying 'entrance'.

Transparency is also important. If a target can be seen from some distance, it allows the visitor to apply direct aiming. Transparency must be coupled with accessibility. The visibility of a main building is not of much help if there is a moat or a motor road without bridges between the visitor and the building. The special needs of physically challenged visitors should also be considered.

The wayshowing hierarchy
1 Environmental clues
2 Direct labels
3 Self-explanation

Figure 49 Some environments are truly self-explanatory. Visitors to the Schönbrunn castle outside Vienna who want to visit the Gloriette in the park surrounding the castle don't need maps or directional signs. They can see their target and the way to it.

49

Wayshowing
Landmarks

Landmarks are environmental anomalies that assist wayfinding. Some landmarks have as their only function to help wayfinding. This applies to lighthouses and other maritime signals. Other landmarks, such as the Eiffel Tower, are primarily made to attract and to be remembered. Finally, some buildings are made with other functions in mind, but they are so conspicuous that they cannot help serving as landmarks. The London Eye Ferris wheel and the 'Gherkin' in London's financial district exemplify this.

Landmarks must meet three conditions. To qualify as landmarks, they must be visible, conspicuous, and easy to talk about. Visibility can in principle be replaced by sounds or radio signals, as in maritime devices, but for the kinds of wayshowing described in W>W, visibility is the key issue.

Landmarks must be more than visible. They must stand out from their surroundings. This implies that landmarks achieve part of their conspicuousness from their context. A very tall building among very tall buildings doesn't stand out, while the same tall building located among low houses would.

It is important that landmarks allow us to talk about them. They must have a name and a character that allow helpful people to say: 'Walk to the Ferris wheel and take the first bridge across the river.' Sculptures and other art manifestations often defy being used as landmarks. The person who wants to show the way doesn't know what to call them, and the wayfarer doesn't know how to recognise them.

Landmarks don't have to be buildings. In an office corridor a coffee machine or a water cooler can serve as a local landmark: 'Dr. Hansen's office? Second door on your right hand after the coffee machine.'

50

51

Figure 50 30 St Mary Axe, London, aka the 'Gherkin'. Design Norman Foster.

Figure 51 Any anomaly, whatever stands out, in the city-, land-, or seascape may serve as a landmark. Rauchfangkehrer (chimney sweep). Wippingerstrasse, Vienna.

Figure 52 The only function of lighthouses and other maritime signals is wayshowing to help wayfinding. Lighthouse. Cape Liptrap, Australia.

Figure 53 The world's most famous sign is a nonagenarian celebrity with its own website. It was born in 1923, and it has probably appeared in more movies and television programs than any actor. The sign originally spelled HOLLYWOODLAND. It was built on Mt. Lee in the Hollywood Hills as a billboard for a real estate development. Since then, the sign has become a true landmark, an icon on par with Mount Rushmore and Times Square. In 1949, the last four letters were dismissed, and in 1978 the 15 metres high sign was demolished and rebuilt. Visitors to www.hollywoodsign.org can see the famous nine letters from a satellite and monitor the 24/7 camera surveillance.

Wayshowing
Toponomy

Names and numbers are tools for thinking. Politicians, planners, and site owners occasionally neglect toponomy, the discipline of giving names to places. They don't realise how helpful this practice can be to wayfinders. They leave place names to whimsical ideas or – worse – political caprice.

As a rule, authors on wayshowing also neglect naming and numbering. Like many designers, they seem to think that these issues are either unimportant or beyond discussion. This is not so. Good language and logical numbering increase navigability. Designers should offer their advice.

With a view to wayshowing, descriptive names are generally preferable to names that are simple designations. Ocean Parkway, Atlantic Boulevard, and Town Hall Square are better names than Anderson Street, Rabbit Boulevard, and Hyacinth Square.

That said, place names that are only designations may have some wayshowing merit if they are thematically clustered. Wayfinders familiar with American literature may understand that Steinbeck Drive, Faulkner Drive, and Dos Passos Drive are situated near each other. Also, perhaps less useful, Little Square hints the existence of a Large Square.

Planners have three choices when giving location-related names to metro stations and other urban transportation nodes. They can name the station after a street, a neighbourhood, or a neighbour. Kensington High Street, Swiss Cottage, and Hyde Park Corner are London underground examples of these three possibilities. Sometimes politicians prefer less logical solutions.

A special problem exists in areas where one language does not fit all. Street signs are bi-lingual English and Gaelic in the Republic of Ireland. Bi-lingual signs using the local language plus a more widespread language are common in airports and other transport terminals in many countries. English seems to be the lingua franca in the world of passenger flying. In regions with two official languages – such as Finnish and Swedish in Finland or Spanish and Catalan in parts of Spain – airport signs may use two local languages plus English to serve both locals and guests.

Assigning numbers to streets, quarters, blocks, houses, floors, and rooms is a special province of toponomy. The two basic requirements of good numbering are logic and consistency. If used in logical ways, numbered facilities will point at each other. If used consistently with the same logic users will learn and use inference when finding their way.

Everybody with the possible exception of wayfinders who suffer from severe acalculia – number blindness – understands that 7th Avenue runs between 6th and 8th Avenue. What street numbers may lack in human touch, they may gain in human value in terms of readability.

Naming buildings (or streets) A, B, C, and so on may simplify wayfinding if the letters are given in alphabetical order. As with numbers, using letters in a logical sequence enables inference.

Some shipping companies don't trust the passengers to remember numbers or letters. As in kindergarten, they call the ferry decks Blue Deck and Red Deck. Some parking houses do the same, and some offer users a paper slip with the relevant identification.

When naming buildings, it is possible to choose between location-related names and occupancy-related names, 'Room 333 in Building C' exemplifies the first principle. 'Maternity Ward' in the 'Women and Children Centre' exemplifies the second principle. The first principle requires no change of signs if the occupants change. The second principle makes it easier for new users to identify the destination.

Giving names to locations sometimes involves a trade-off between emotion and rationality. 'Cancer ward' sounds brutal to patients and their families. Nevertheless, it is more understandable than 'Oncology ward', a term that has the same meaning to physicians. Nobody understands what a department called '2K' means, but they may understand that it lies between '2J' and '2L' on second floor.

Floor designations should preferably take their starting point at the level of the main entrance. Buildings with street entrances on more than one level create problems. Floors below street level are sometimes numbered with a minus prefix. This is an easily misunderstood solution. 'U' is a preferable prefix in English and German speaking countries. Different geographical regions have different conventions for numbering floors.

It may be a good idea to let the floor number be the first part of a room number. When given the keys to our hotel room, we intuitively expect to find room 2202 on the 22nd floor. This principle can be expanded to comprise the building, then A2202 stands for room two on the 22nd floor of building A. Alphanumeric designation is an option for all kinds of site numbering.

Room numbering systems should preferably be open systems, able to adapt to later additions of rooms without spoiling the logic.

Instead of being designated A, B, or C, buildings or building parts can sometimes refer to compass directions such as West Wing, South Gallery, and North Tower.

Sign planners sometimes reinforce the numbering of blocks, floors, and rooms by assigning different colours to different parts of the building. The value of this redundant information is often debatable. Will it provide more confusion than understanding?

The streets of this city have no names. This domiciliary obliteration seems inconvenient to those (like us) who have been used to asserting that the most practical is always the most rational (a principle by virtue of which the best urban toponomy would be that of numbered streets as in the United States and in Kyoto, a Chinese ((sic!)) city).
Roland Barthes about Tokyo in *Empire of Signs*.

Figure 54 House number telling a story. The buoy is a visual pun on the original occupant's name: Kay Bojesen, silversmith. Copenhagen.

Figure 55 Room numbers in this London hotel do not facilitate the inference wayfinding strategy. Not all room numbers indicate the floor. Rooms in the same hundreds are located on different floors. Some rooms on one floor have higher numbers than rooms on a higher floor.

54

PRESS BUTTON	FLOOR INDICATOR	
3	3rd Floor	Rooms 255-281
2	2nd Floor	Rooms 230-254, & 305-322
1	1st Floor	Rooms 205-229, & 283-304
R	Dining Room, Lounge Bar	
M	Mezzanine Floor	Rooms 200-202 Mezzanine Room Basil Room, Korany Room
G	Ground Floor	Porter's Desk, Reception Office, Parrot Club
B	Basement	

55

Wayshowing
Signs

Although we would rather do without them, wayshowing signs are in many ways the most important wayshowing aid. When the edifice has been designed, erected, and maybe taken into use, signs are very often the only wayshowing aid at hand. Signs are also the most flexible wayshowing aid, and they often make up for mistakes in planning. The importance of signs together with their countless different functions and forms, explain why the major part of *W>W* deals with sign design.

Wayshowing signs show the way, and much more. They show locations and give information about locations.

Identification signs state the name, function, or nature of a location.

Directional signs show the way to something, which – in principle – cannot be seen from the location of the signs.

Description signs give all kinds of information that help the wayfinder: building occupants, office hours, flight departures, etc.

Regulation signs deal with commands and prohibitions that affect safety, security, and the practical use of a location.

Signs may be static or dynamic. As the iconic split-flap displays in airports and railway stations disappear, all dynamic signs are electronic.

Maps can be considered a special kind of sign. They are dealt with separately in the following section.

The three following chapters deal with sign theory, sign functions, and sign contents respectively.

56
57
58

Figure 56 Identification sign. London.

Figure 57 Description sign. Canterbury Shaker Village, USA.

Figure 58 Regulation sign. Santa Barbara, USA.

Figure 59 Directional signs. Gamla Stan, Stockholm.

60 W>W

Kungliga Slottet
The Royal Palace

Isskulpturer
Ice Sculptures

STORES
RESTAURANTS
GALLERIES

← 80m
WC

Wayshowing
Maps

Planar maps are two-dimensional pictorial representations of a three-dimensional world. They depict the world in a reduced scale, excluding everything but selected features. Maps are defined by the way they deal with three abstractions: projection, scale, and signatures.

Projection designates the way the spherical world is depicted on a flat map.

Scale designates the size ratio between the map and the real world. On a 1:20,000 map one centimetre represents twenty thousand centimetres or 200 metres.

Signatures are the graphic SIGNS* that stand for all kinds of real world phenomena, such as churches, roads, railway lines, mountains, rivers, and woods.

Cartographers distinguish among maps that deal with land, charts that deal with seas, and plans that deal with cities and buildings. We shall deal with maps and plans. As non-cartographers, we shall follow common usage and refer to plans as maps. Nobody talks about 'you-are-here plans', but 'you-are-here maps', whether they deal with landscape, urban, or indoor areas.

Graphic designers sometimes distinguish between maps and diagrams. In this case, maps are topographical maps, while diagrams stand for such structural maps as transit maps issued by metros. Here too, we shall follow common usage and sometimes refer to these diagrams as maps.

In terms of wayshowing, portable – handheld – maps and y-a-h maps are the relevant categories. Portable maps are used as an off-location medium that wayfinders can study before departure and take with them to find their way on a journey. Y-a-h maps are placed in the environment, which they describe. Their location is generally marked with a you-are-here symbol on the map. It is important that the map users can establish their exact position by comparing the map with the view. Sign planners should facilitate this comparison by including easily recognisable features on the map.

* In W>W, the word 'SIGN' written with upper case letters stands for anything that carries a meaning. The word 'sign' written with lower case letters stands for graphic messages in the environment that help wayfinders to get around.

Figure 60 Transit maps are designed for train riding rather than walking. As a rule, they distort distances to achieve better readability and space economy. Metropolitana Milanese, Metro. Milan.

Figure 61 The usability of a y-a-h map depends on the marking of the exact location of the map. The Chinese Wall authorities unfortunately forgot to place the y-a-h star on the map.

60

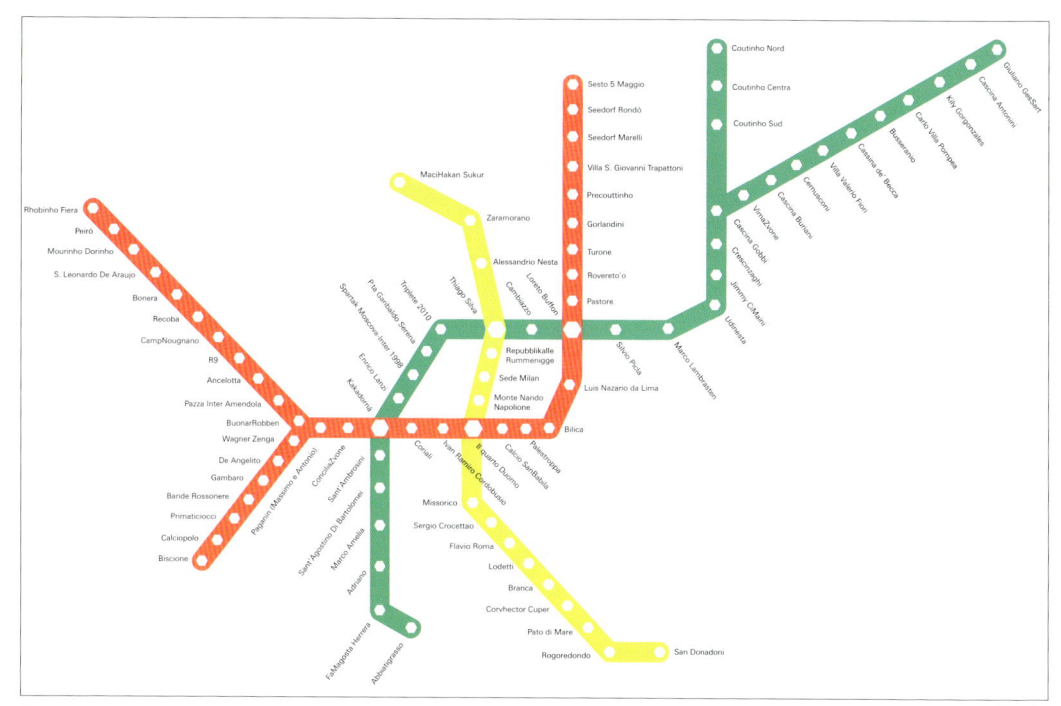

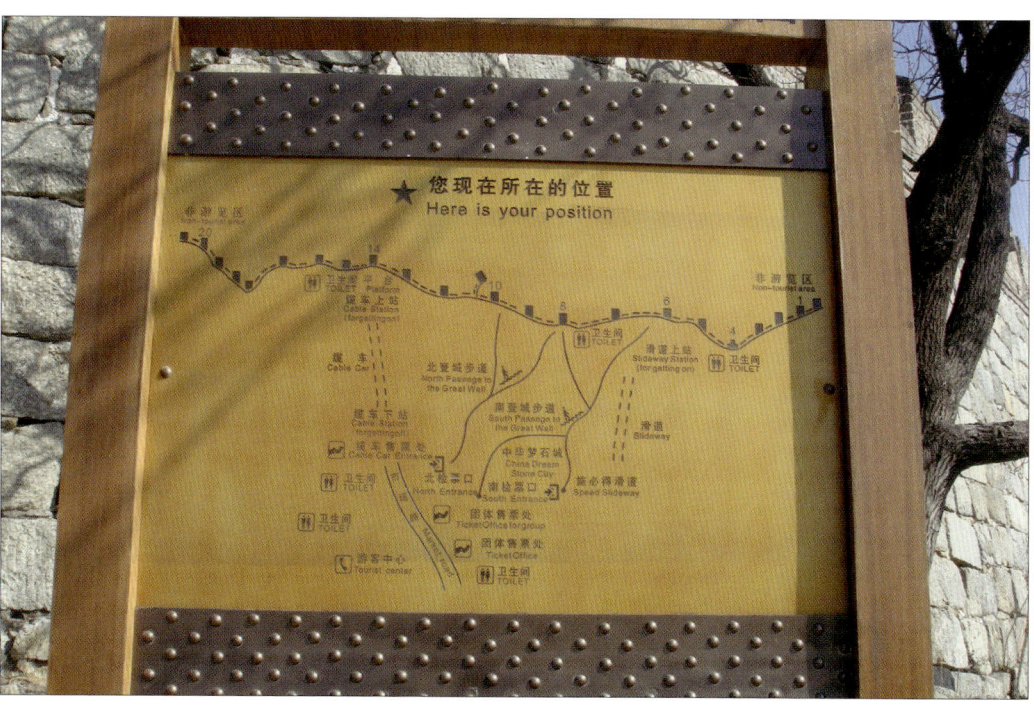

61

W>W 63

Maps

Both portable maps and y-a-h maps can be area maps or route maps. Area maps describe a designated area, while route maps concentrate on a specific route through an area.

Maps are small graphic abstractions of reality. They edit reality by showing selected features and omitting other features. What is shown and what is omitted depend on the purpose of the map. What is omitted is as important as what is shown. Too many features confuse the map reader. Map design is always a trade-off between information load and clarity. Maps with more information may be less informative.

Maps facilitate wayfinding. Area maps facilitate sense-making while route maps facilitate rule-following. To benefit from sense-making, the reader must invest time in learning. These efforts are rewarded with a deeper understanding and perhaps a choice of routes leading to the desired goal.

Y-a-h maps are most often shown vertically. There are practical reasons for this. A vertical map will not be used as table and it will not collect dirt or snow. A vertical map is better noticed, and more easily read from a distance. On the other hand, a correctly oriented horizontal map is easier to read.

Two principles determine the orientation of a vertically positioned map.

Principle one means following the tradition of north up and south down. Text on maps favours this.

Principle two is forward-up-alignment, aka forward-up-equivalence, or head-up. What is up on the map is forward in the environment.

To follow both principles at the same time implies that a vertically placed map must face south. Wayfinders looking at the map will face north while having both north and forward up on the map. Ideally, vertically placed maps should face south. However, this rule may be relaxed in some situations.

62

Figure 62 Road sign with map. Denmark.

Figure 63 You-are-here map. Rikshospitalet, Oslo. Design Mollerup Designlab.

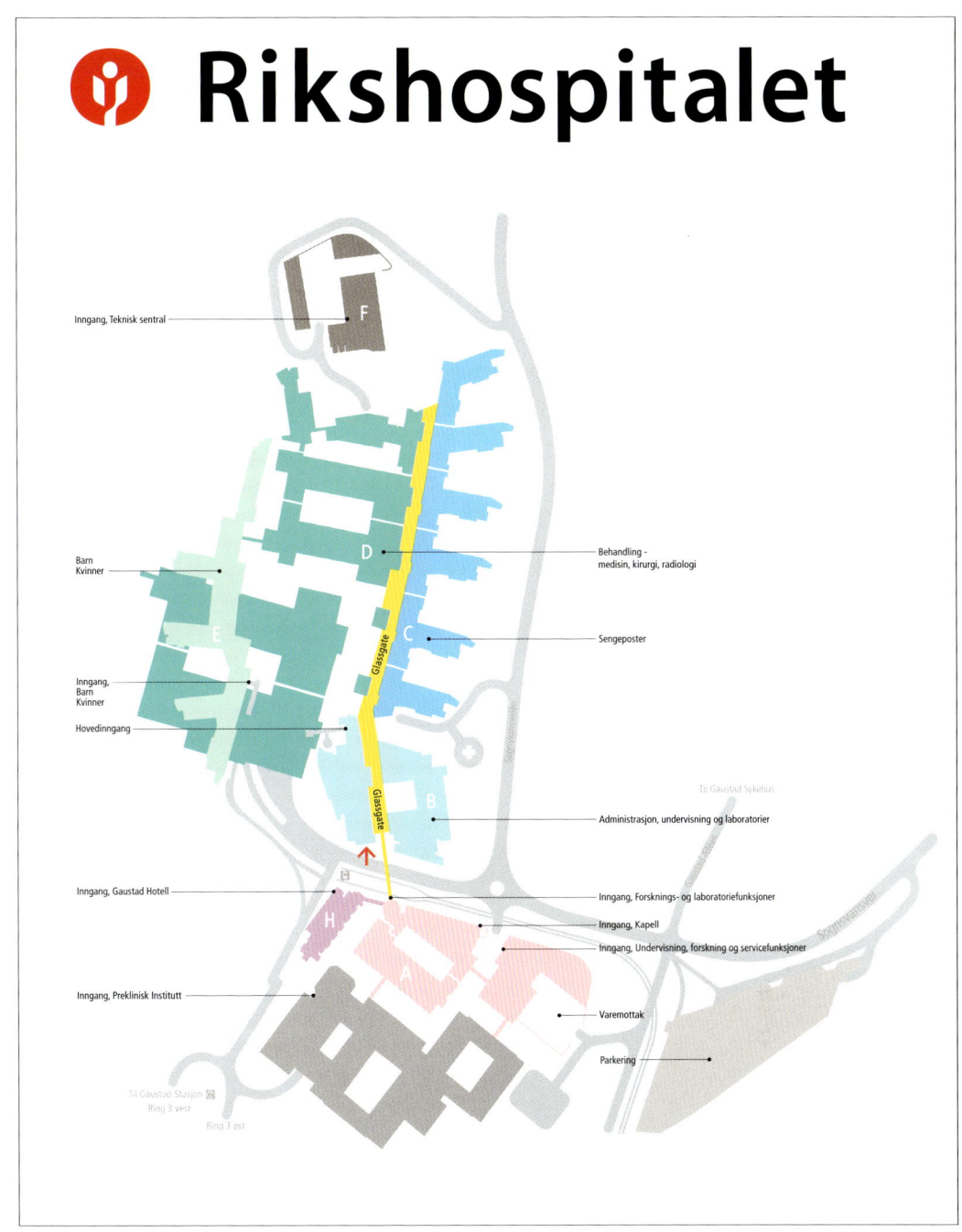

Rikshospitalet

Inngang, Teknisk sentral

Barn Kvinner

Behandling - medisin, kirurgi, radiologi

Sengeposter

Inngang, Barn Kvinner

Hovedinngang

Administrasjon, undervisning og laboratorier

Inngang, Gaustad Hotell

Inngang, Forsknings- og laboratoriefunksjoner

Inngang, Kapell

Inngang, Undervisning, forskning og servicefunksjoner

Inngang, Preklinisk Institutt

Varemottak

Parkering

Wayshowing
Help desks

However well a complex environment is planned and signposted, there will always be wayfinders who lose their way or prefer to get wayfinding information from a human being. These people hope to find a manned information counter. Such counters give oral information and sometimes issue personalised route maps.

Information counters typically give other kinds of information than wayshowing, which for practical reasons cannot be given by signs and other media. Such information may deal with all kinds of issues concerning the function of the place in question. In fact, at most information counters in airports, hospitals, fairs, and elsewhere, wayshowing is only a minor part of information services.

Some venues have clearly identified information officers patrolling areas where most visitors need help.

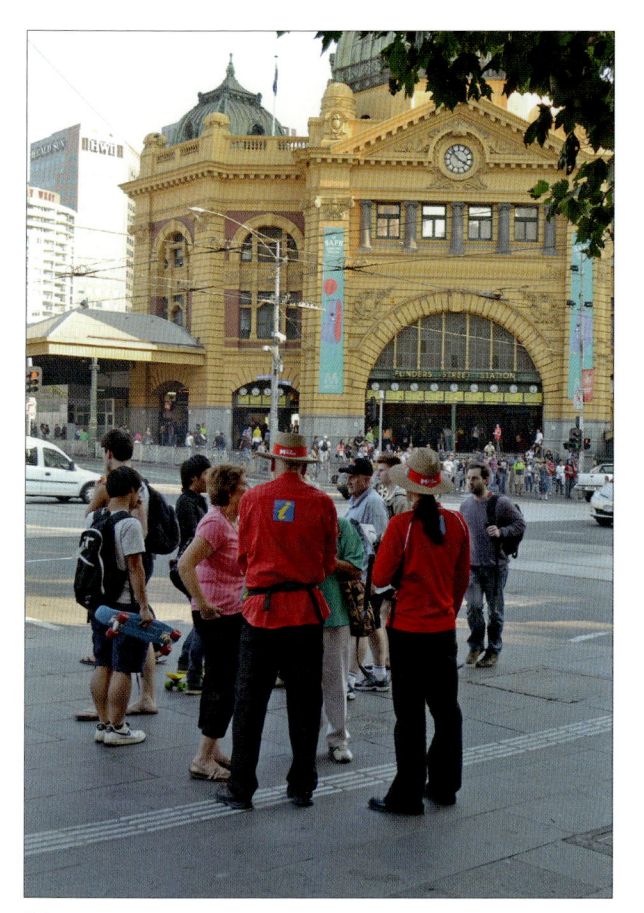

Figure 64 Information officers. Melbourne.

Figure 65 Help point, subway. New York.

Figure 66 Information counter, Melbourne Convention and Exhibition Centre.

Figure 67 adidas research and development building 'adidas Laces'. Herzogenaurach, Germany. Design büro uebele.

64

65

66
67

Wayshowing
Pre-visit information

To paraphrase Louis Pasteur, wayfinding favours the prepared mind. Most wayfinders can benefit from studying websites and printed material with maps and verbal descriptions before visiting a new complex environment.

For example, pre-visit information sent by a hospital together with an appointment can be helpful in several ways:

First, pre-visit information can help the patient to plan his visit: which public transportation to use, or where to park, which entrance to use, how to find the relevant department, where to report.

Second, the wayfinder can take a printed map or a verbal description along with him and use as a guide.

Third, pre-visit information can give a more or less detailed idea about the area to be visited and inform the wayfinder's mental map.

Patients and other visitors given pre-visit information make fewer demands on the hospital staff by finding their way without stopping every white coat they meet and by being in time for their appointment.

Personalise pre-visit information when possible.

Figure 68 Graphic designer Mette Heinz sent this map to prospective visitors in Talbot Road.

Figure 69 On their website Heathrow Airport informs users how to approach and park.

68

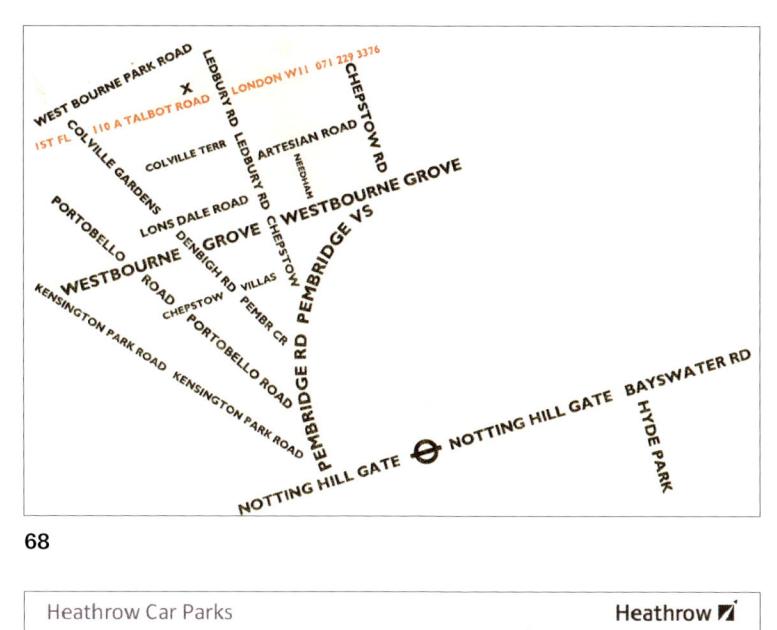

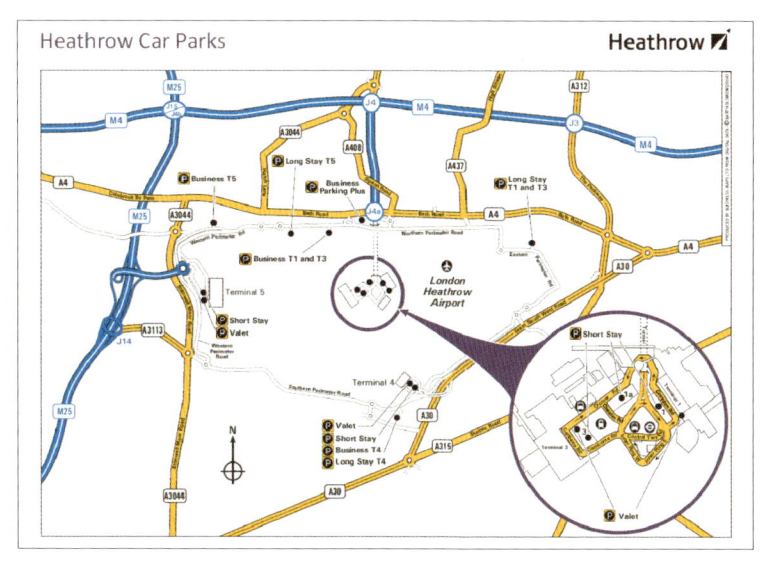

69

Wayshowing
Simplicity vs. redundancy

Two contrasting principles must be balanced against each other in all wayshowing projects. These are simplicity and redundancy.

Simplicity in wayshowing includes simplicity of principles, elements, number of sign types, number of signs, and number of sizes. The functional goal of simplicity is to increase the navigability by offering clarity and avoiding clutter. Travellers shouldn't be confused or overwhelmed by signs and other wayshowing aids that are too complex, too many, or too large. The aesthetic desire to keep an environment as clean and quiet as possible also points to simplicity. Finally, costs also encourage restraint in signposting.

Redundancy in information is information given more than once. It is 'superfluous' information that is – to some degree – useful. A message with no redundancy is vulnerable to noise, errors, and misunderstanding.

A loudspeaker message in a traffic terminal just saying 'line E' may in principle appear very clear. But to some passengers it might be heard as 'line D'. 'Line E to Harrington' is a longer message and the to-Harrington part is redundant if line E always goes to Harrington. However, the redundant information may clarify the message to some passengers.

A small airport with two piers, each with ten gates, may name the system in three different ways:

– Numbering the gates 1 through 20 is the most simple and most vulnerable way. Did the loudspeaker say 'gate seven' or 'gate eleven'?

– Numbering the gates A1 through A10 and B1 through B10 will probably send more passengers in the right direction. The 'superfluous' addition of pier designation helps passengers finding the right direction.

– Finally, numbering the gates A1 through A10 and B11 through B20 adding both the pier designation and using larger numbers than necessary is the most fail proof solution.

Would the wayfinding be still more effective if signs relating to A1 through A10 were green and signs relating to B11 through B20 were blue? Probably not. Too many types of information may confuse rather than inform. Enough is enough. The balance between simplicity and redundancy calls for delicate attention.

The above examples deal with naming train lines and airport piers. But the question of simplicity vs. redundancy exists in – and between – all kinds of wayshowing aids. How often should directional signs be repeated on the way to a distant destination? Do we need loudspeaker departure calls if there are good visual signs?

Not all redundant information qualifies as useful. Much redundant information is just superfluous. In wayshowing, the difference between useful redundancy and the merely superfluous is often a judgment call.

Practical theory

To many people, the term 'practical theory' is an oxymoron – a self-contradicting expression similar to 'eloquent silence' or 'make haste slowly'. This is because we often see practice and theory presented as opposites – acting versus thinking. However, theory may be more academic, or less, and it may be useful in the real world. The semiotic and communication theory presented in this chapter has clear relevance to solving practical wayshowing problems.

Practical theory
A theory of signs

Practitioners in the sign trade presumably don't spend their day speculating about a theory of signs. Making signage that works is a practical occupation in which experience, refined by learning from mistakes, teaches what is not immediately clear to the beginner. But useful theories do exist for signage. Although their originators did not think specifically about signage, some SIGN and communication theories apply to the business of signage. These theories expand our understanding of practical phenomena and offer guidelines for good signage practice. The distance between theory and practice is short.

Theory deals with the analysis of facts and their relations. The communication and SIGN theories presented in this chapter deal with facts about SIGNS and relations among SIGNS and the way they work. The section *Messages* considers SIGNS according to the sender's intentions. What does the sender want to accomplish with his communication? The section *Signification* deals with SIGNS according to the relation between what they show and what they stand for. *Levels of communication* analyses SIGNS according to their impact on the receiver.
Finally, *Why signs don't work* demonstrates how the shortcomings of dysfunctional signage can be explained on theoretical grounds. Theory has much to offer wayshowing practitioners.

Practical theory
Messages

Messages are chunks of information transmitted from a sender to a receiver. French semiologist Pierre Guiraud suggests three different modes of communication: indication, representation, and injunction. They deal with being, knowing, and acting respectively. In *W>W*, we shall rename Guiraud's three categories for a practical theory of signs: identification, explanation, and instruction.

Three modes of communication

Guiraud's terms	Our terms
– indication	– identification
– representation	– explanation
– injunction	– instruction

Three signs in an airport exemplify the three modes of communication:

– The sign text 'Tickets' is an example of identification. The sign identifies the ticket office.

– The sign text 'Tickets' together with an arrow is an example of explanation. The sign explains in what direction the ticket office is found.

– The sign text 'No smoking' is an example of instruction. The sign instructs the reader to do something, to refrain from smoking.

The messages in these three examples are objective. They are not coloured by the sender's feelings; they address the reader's intellect and call for understanding. Wayshowing signs depend directly on their objective qualities to be useful. Other messages may be less objective and more subjective. They address the reader's feelings and call for participation.

Later, we shall further refine the tripartite division of communication modes in terms of sign messages. This classification helps the practical planning of signs.

Pierre Guiraud
Semiology
Routledge, London, 1975

70
71
72

Figure 70 The floor number sign tells that you are on the seventh floor of the GS (George Swinburne) building. It identifies. Swinburne University of Technology. Melbourne.

Figure 71 The directional sign shows the way to the rest rooms. It explains. Swinburne University of Technology. Melbourne.

Figure 72 The pictogram says what to do: Refrain from leaning out. It instructs. Swinburne University of Technology. Melbourne.

Practical theory
Signification

Signs are also SIGNS in the broad meaning of the word. Because of its general qualities, the study of SIGNS throws light on the nature and function of signs. This section deals with signification, the relation between what a SIGN shows and what it stands for. In semiotic jargon: the relation between signifier and signified.

A SIGN with a natural relation between signifier and signified, between what it shows and what it means, is a motivated SIGN. A sign showing a pair of spectacles outside an optician's shop is a motivated SIGN. It is immediately understandable.

A SIGN with no natural relation between signifier and signified is an arbitrary SIGN. A non-figurative trademark sign outside a bank is an arbitrary sign. An arbitrary sign is only understandable because of a convention, an agreement about meaning.

With respect to signification, SIGNS are classified as icons, indices*, and symbols. Icons and indices are motivated SIGNS. Symbols are arbitrary SIGNS. The classification serves as a guide to the questions, which planners should ask in practical situations: Is the motivation strong enough to secure immediate understanding? Is the lack of motivation compensated by a strong convention?

*'Indices' is plural of 'index' when used in semiotics. Otherwise it is 'indexes'.

<u>Three classes of SIGNS</u>
- icons   – motivated
- indices   – motivated
- symbols   – arbitrary

Practical theory
Icons

An icon is a SIGN related to its object by similarity. The signifier and the signified – what is shown, and what is meant – share some quality. This makes the icon a motivated SIGN.

The wine merchant's trademark showing a bunch of grapes is an icon. By definition, icons are easily decodable. They show directly what they mean. The relation between signifier and signified is obvious.

Icons may be divided into three subclasses:

Classes of icons
- images
- diagrams
- metaphors

Images are icons that simply picture their object. The wine merchant's bunch of grapes is an image. So is the electrician's giant plug sign.

Diagrams are visual abstractions that have a structural similarity to their objects. The electrician's mark illustrating direct and alternate current is a diagram.

Metaphors are icons that share one or more conceptual qualities with their object. Lufthansa's stylised bird logo is a metaphor, the shared quality is flying.

73
74
75

Figure 73 Icon/image: Signifier and signified are related to each other by one-to-one symbolism. An electrician's giant plug sign. Copenhagen.

Figure 74 Icon/diagram: The signifier has a structural similarity with the signified. Danish electrician's mark illustrating direct and alternate current. Copenhagen.

Figure 75 Icon/metaphor: The signifier shares a conceptual quality – flying – with the signified. Lufthansa.

76 W>W

Practical theory
Indices

An index relates to its object by some kind of obvious physical relation. It is a motivated SIGN. Indices may be divided into two classes:

Classes of indices
- designations
- reagents

Designations point physically to their object. All spatial signs are designations by definition. They point to and derive part of their meaning from their location. The horse butcher's horsehead sign offers its generic meaning – horse butcher – to its location. The specific location adds 'here' to the message. Together, the sign and the place say: 'Here is a horse butcher.'

Reagents are related to their object by causal relationships. The object is the cause. The SIGN is the effect. The pastry smell from a bakery is a reagent. The bakery is the cause. The smell is the effect. Again the relation is double. The generic smell says baker. The specific location says which baker. The good smell inside and outside the baker's shop is probably incidental – accepted rather than intended. In the same way, the music heard outside a shop selling musical instruments or recorded music may be more or less unintentional.

On the other hand, the generous way in which perfumeries in department stores disseminate their fragrances seems to be planned. The olfactory SIGN is an intentional reagent. Some shops selling trendy sailor's style clothing to landlubbers go a step further and condition the shop atmosphere with the seductive smell of tar. In this case, smell is a simulated reagent.

76

Figure 76 All spatial signs work indexically: they achieve part of their meaning through their location. The horsehead says more than 'horse butcher'. It says: 'Here is a horse butcher.' Le Marais, Paris.

Practical theory
Symbols

While icons and indices are motivated SIGNS, symbols are arbitrary SIGNS. Signifier and signified are related to each other by convention. A convention can be formal or informal. In the case of mathematical symbols, the convention is formal. Mathematical conventions are the result of professional agreement within the discipline. In the case of obscene finger gestures, the convention is informal. These gestures are the result of a common understanding among the members of specific cultural groups.

Motivated SIGNS and arbitrary SIGNS are not absolute. The receiver's culture shapes the meaning. A pawnbroker's sign is arbitrary to the passersby who don't know why the pawnbroker uses three golden balls as his shop sign. To those who know that the three golden balls refer to the arms of the Medici, an Italian dynasty of bankers, the balls are a motivated SIGN. If some people think that the three balls signify pool room they practice what Umberto Eco calls 'aberrant decoding'.

The three categories of SIGNS – icons, indices, and symbols – are not mutually exclusive. In some countries, a baker's pretzel is an icon depicting the bakery products. It is also an index that gets part of its meaning through location. Finally, it is a symbol: In some areas, bakers herald their presence with the sign of a pretzel by common convention.

Figure 77 The HSBC logo is an arbitrary sign, it's a symbol.

Figure 78 The baker's pretzel is three things in one: an icon, an index, and a symbol. Bergen, Norway.

Figure 79 Pawnbroker. An icon/metaphor to those who understand the Medici connection, and a symbol to those who don't. Chalk Farm Road, London.

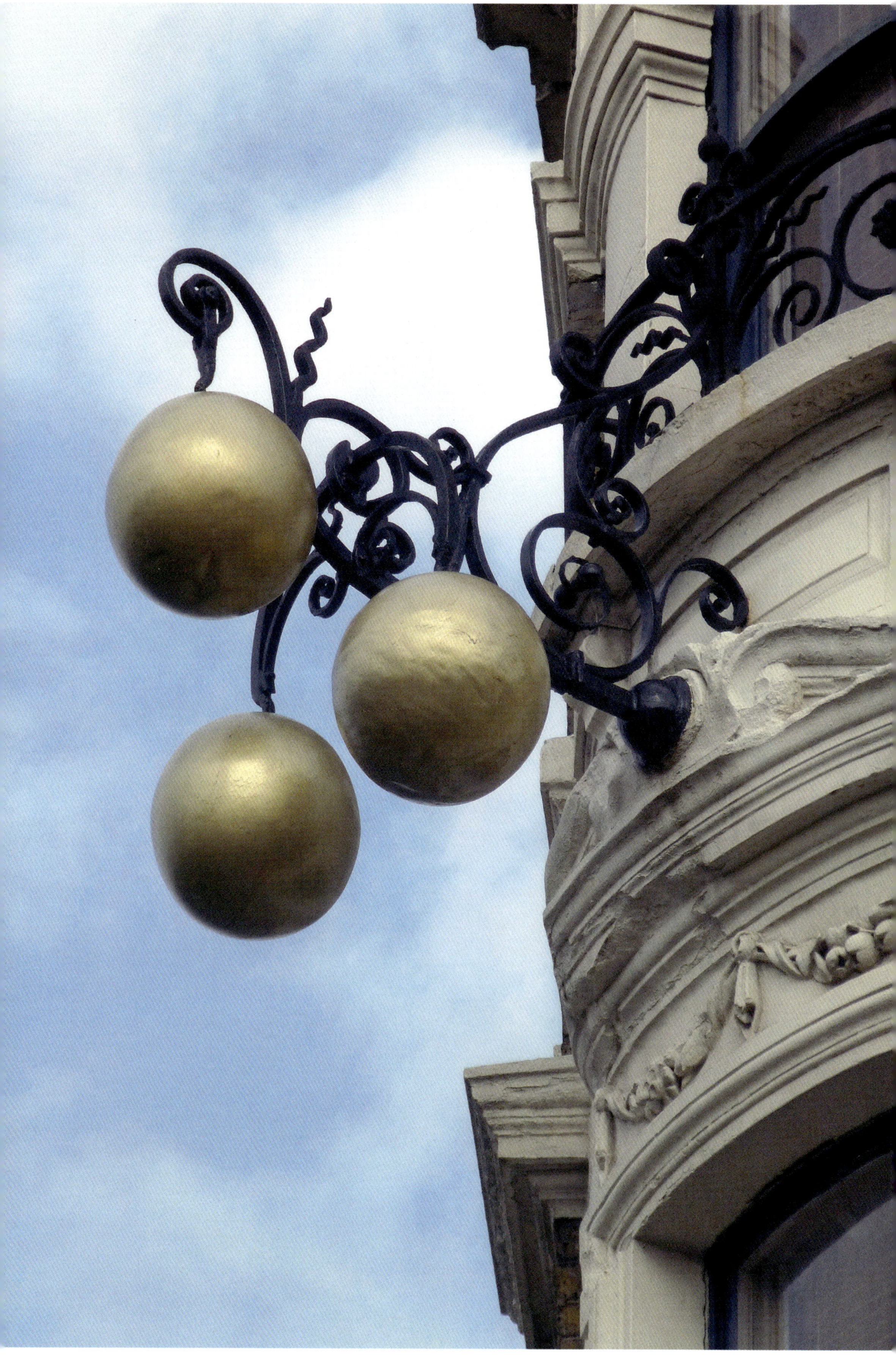

79

Practical theory
Levels of communication

This section deals with the impact of a SIGN on the receiver.

The impact of a SIGN may be discussed on three levels originally suggested by Claude E. Shannon and Warren Weaver in *The Mathematical Theory of Communication,* from 1949. These are the technical level, the semantic level, and the effectiveness level.

Claude E. Shannon & Warren Weaver
The Mathematical Theory of Communication
The Illinois University Press, Urbana, 1949

On the technical level, the message of a sign is seen as a signal that can be received more or less correctly. On the technical level, the relevant quality is legibility, the distinctness that makes perception easy.

On the semantic level, the message is seen as a carrier of meaning that can be understood more or less correctly. On the semantic level, the relevant qualities are readability and comprehensibility that make the message easy to read and understand.

On the effectiveness level, the message is seen as a means of influencing the behaviour of the receiver. On the effectiveness level, the relevant quality is persuasiveness, the power of a message to convince receivers.

Level of communication	Relevant quality
– technical level	– legibility
– semantic level	– comprehensibility
– effectiveness level	– persuasiveness

A road sign, a circular white disc with a red border and black text '60 km', may exemplify the three levels of communication.

The sign functions on the technical level, if motor drivers can clearly see and read the sign from the intended distance while approaching at traffic speed.

The sign also functions on the semantic level, if motor drivers understand what the message means: until further notice the maximum speed is 60 kilometres per hour.

Finally, the sign functions on the effectiveness level if drivers – having seen and understood the sign – continue at a maximum speed of 60 kilometres per hour. The sign has failed on the effectiveness level if drivers proceed at 70 kilometres per hour (unless sign planners have calculated for a 10 kilometres per hour measure of standard civil disobedience).

Konrad Lorenz was in line with Shannon and Weaver when he suggested that saying something is not the same as being heard, that being heard is not the same as being understood, and that being understood is not the same as convincing somebody.

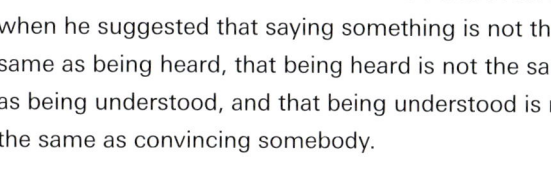

Check that all SIGNS work technically, semantically, and effectively.

Figure 80 Road sign 60 km/h.

Figure 81 Suggestive German road sign on the Autobahn where there is no general speed limit.

Practical theory
Why signs don't work

Signs work or don't work because they comply or don't comply with the simple theoretical principles outlined in this chapter.

Sometimes signs don't work because they simply don't exist. Sometimes the identity of a building is more or less hidden. Only close neighbours and regular users know that the building on the square is a public office. Perhaps no signs guide citizens to the right office. Perhaps no signs inform visitors what they must do and what they must refrain from doing. The public office lacks signs that identify, explain, and instruct.

Signs frequently don't work because they don't function on the technical level. This happens when they are not visible or legible from the proper positions. Presumptive users cannot spot them and read them. Perhaps the signs are too small or located too far away or located in an otherwise wrong position. Perhaps the signs are covered by plants or by other signs. Perhaps they are not kept clean and tidy. Perhaps they are ageing and decomposing.

Sometimes signs don't work, because there is too little colour contrast between the signboard and its surroundings or too little contrast between the letters, pictograms, or arrows and the signboard. Sometimes signs are so glossy that glare hinders fast and reliable reading. Sometimes loose letters mounted at a distance from the wall cast shadows that mingle with the letter shapes to make the sign unreadable.

Signs may be perfectly visible and still not function as intended because intended readers don't understand them. The signs don't work on the semantic level. Perhaps sign readers don't know the language of the sign. Perhaps the readers do understand the language, but don't understand the unclear text. The text is not comprehensible. Not all relevant users of a hospital know what urology is. A lot of pictograms don't work as intended because the images do not resemble what they should. They are neither motivated nor supported by a strong convention.

82

83

Figure 82 Last come, first seen, seems to be the ruling principle here. Paris.

Figure 83-85 Green is great, but not in front of signs. Copenhagen.

84
85

Why signs don't work

Sometimes signs are positioned wrongly and thereby lose their indexical meaning. They lack the power of position.

Signs may be visible, correctly positioned, and perfectly understandable but they still may not work. That is the case when the signs function on the technical and semantic levels without functioning on the effectiveness level. They are seen and understood but they fail to convince. This is fortunately the case with much advertising, and – less fortunately – the case with many public signs including such signs as 'No smoking', 'No mobile phones', 'No hawking', 'No bikes in the park'. For one reason or another, many sign readers seem to think that this type of message does not apply to them.

Use SIGN theory to control sign functionality.

Figure 86-88 Too little colour contrast.

Figure 86 Gold is not the gold standard in signage when used for both letters and background. The colour contrast is too little. The Trump Tower on Fifth Avenue in New York demonstrates this.

Figure 87 Copenhagen.

Figure 88 Museum Moderner Kunst. MuseumsQuartier, Vienna.

Figure 89 Elegant? Not readable.

86

84 W>W

87
88
89

W>W 85

Sign functions

Signs for wayshowing cover four different messages: identification, direction, description, and regulation. Understanding the differences between these categories and their functional requirements is vital to good wayshowing design.

Sign functions
Sign categories

Environmental signs state something related to their location. According to their function, environmental signs may be classified into four categories. This classification represents a functional refinement of the three part division suggested in the Messages section. The two divisions compare in the following way:

Three part division	Four part division
– identification	– identification
– explanation	– direction
	– description
– instruction	– regulation

Identification signs identify a certain position or something located at that position. '290 Park Avenue', 'Seagram Building', and 'Four Seasons Restaurant' are three examples of identification sign messages.

Directional signs say what will be found in the direction indicated. A short text supplied with an arrow is the standard content of directional signs.

Descriptive signs describe the state of affairs at a certain location. Signs with business hours and directories of large buildings belong to this category.

Regulatory signs are sometimes referred to as 'command and prohibition signs'. They regulate the use of an area with a view to safety, security, and utility. 'No admittance', 'Hard hat area', and 'Members only' are text examples of this category.

Environmental signs relate to their surroundings in a way that excludes pure advertising. However, the four categories mentioned here may all include commercial elements.

It has sometimes been suggested that the difference between commercial and non-commercial signs is that commercial signs persuade while non-commercial signs inform. That is a truth with limitations. All commercial signs inform and many non-commercial signs include elements of persuasion.

Sign categories

Another difference between commercial and non-commercial signage is the energy invested in commercial signage. A hotdog stand, which is more eye-catchingly signposted than the city hall, in front of which it stands, is a case in point. Most of the time, a sign's general appearance – size, typographic arrangement, colour, and other graphic elements – reveals whether the sign is commercial or not. When commercial signs are not limited by strict rules, they tend to steal the show from non-commercial signs.

In principle, *W>W* will only deal with commercial signs that relate to place. Shop signs belong to this category. Advertising boards don't.

Classifying sign functions in four categories allows us to study similarities and differences among signs to better understand their function.

Signs can belong to more than one category. A sign stating 'The ice is not safe' is an explicit descriptive sign. At the same time it contains an implicit regulatory message that says 'Stay away from the ice'. The classical 'Cave canem!', 'Beware of the dog!', is nothing but a classic euphemism for saying 'Stay away from my property'.

Figure 90 Commercial signs come in many flavours. Lisbon.

ESPINGARDAS
REVOLWERS
PISTOLAS
CARGAS
E
Todos os accessorios
PARA
CAÇADORES

ARTIGOS
PARA
ESGRIMA

Sign functions
Identification

Identification means establishing identity. The identity of a place includes all the qualities that belong to it and make it different from other places. For the purpose of communication, the name of the place represents all these qualities.

The business of identification signs is stating the names of places. Names of places can be pure toponymic designations*: 'The North Pole', '10 Downing Street', or 'Suite 2002'. Names of places can also refer to what is found at the location: 'Museum of Modern Art', 'Nike Town', or the name or business of any organisation, company, or person at a certain place.

*The word 'designation' is here used in its ordinary meaning, and should not be mistaken for designation as an index category. *See page 77.*

By establishing the identity of a place, a sign says what the place is or what is found there. To some degree, it also says what the place is not or what is not found there. A doorplate saying 'Smith, Smith, and Smith Law Firm' states that the company sells legal assistance but probably not diving gear or snow scooters.

As other messages do, identification signs achieve part of their meaning from their context. The meaning of an identification sign is qualified by its location. The place says where to find what the sign announces.

Apart from the simple geographic information, the message can get an expanded meaning from its place. A neon sign 'Nyhavn 17' located in a street stuffed with bars and restaurants does more than repeat the street address. Supported by the type of lettering the context explains the nature of the establishment.

91
92

The identification sign in front of Restaurant L'Escargot near the Centre Pompidou in Paris also does a lot more than denoting the linguistic message. The elaborate façade in the old style connotes traditional French cooking, tables laid with heavy white tablecloths, waiters with long white aprons, wooden panels, large mirrors, and so on. This is not a place for backpackers.

Figure 91-93 The signs reveal the type of establishment.

Figure 91 L'Escargot. Paris.

Figure 92 Nyhavn 17. Copenhagen.

Figure 93 Non-verbal identification sign. Luna Park. Melbourne.

The understanding of a sign is also conditioned by the culture of the sign reader. Educated users read the sign 'New York Bar Association' in the lobby of a New York office building as the name of the powerful organisation of lawyers and judges. To sign readers with different background the text might be understood as the name of an organisation of tavern owners. The culture of the sign reader shapes understanding or lack of understanding.

Sign functions
Direction

Directional signs recommend a route from the position of the sign to the destination given on the sign. As other spatial signs do, directional signs function indexically. They derive part of their meaning from their location. In fact, directional signs are double or triple coded. One part of the meaning of a directional sign derives from its location. Another part of its meaning is given by the direction to which it points. A third part of the meaning may be contained in text or pictures that tell what can be found in the indicated direction.

The rule that understanding signs depends on context particularly applies to directional signs. They tie 'here' and 'there' together. The context may more or less convincingly support the message of the sign.

In some cases, context makes the sign redundant. The sign may be superfluous if the target is clearly visible and identifiable from the position of the sign.

The generic graphic SIGN of direction is the image of an arrow. But other images are used to show direction, such as the image of a pointing hand. A white running man on a green background is the official directional sign for escape route. The destination is 'away from this building'.

Sometimes directional signs have no text and consist only of images. Escape route signs are normally used without text. Intended users are expected to know the convention. Solitary arrows are most often seen as road signs, where they are probably not directional signs in the way the term is used here. A solitary arrow in traffic typically expresses a command and a prohibition rather than an explanation how to get to a certain destination. It means 'drive in that direction' and it means 'do not drive in the opposite direction'. The directional traffic arrow is as much a regulatory sign as a directional sign.

In most situations other than traffic, directional images, primarily arrows, are qualified by an explanatory text: 'To the trains', 'Observatory', 'Aix les Bains', 'Toutes directions', 'Gents'.

In some cases, directional signs work with text alone. The text 'To the aircraft' over a door in an airport terminal directs without further explanation. In fact, any door with an identification sign functions as a directional sign. A special kind of directional sign is the kind of coloured line on the floor sometimes used at hospitals where staff members say 'follow the red line to the X-ray department' instead of giving complicated route descriptions.

The red carpet rolled out in front of cinemas and town halls to announce and welcome celebrities doubles as homage and as a directional sign. In a confusing environment with photoflashes, nosy reporters, and noisy crowds, the red carpet frees the guests of honour from wayfinding problems.

Figure 94 Fingerpost. Royal Botanic Gardens, Sydney.

Figure 95 Multiple choice. Moorfields Saddle, Australia.

Sign functions
Description

Descriptive signs explain something about the situation at their location. This enables sign readers to act on a more informed level than they would otherwise do. Some descriptive signs simply explain what is found at their place. Directories listing the tenants of an office building and their location exemplify this.

Descriptive signs dealing with time constitute a special category. This includes static signs stating office hours, dynamic signs in a hotel lobby listing the day's events, as well as dynamic room signs.

Strictly speaking, many descriptive signs don't deal with wayshowing as such. They deal with placeshowing. That is the case with the signs that show departure and arrival times in the metro or the airport and it applies to the signs that explain the content of a museum. To the user, the need for these different kinds of information often accompanies a need for wayfinding. Sometimes, the obvious design for wayshowing and placeshowing is a seamless wall-to-wall solution. At other times, there is good reason in keeping signage for wayshowing and placeshowing apart.

A special category of descriptive signs includes signs that tell the distance to some remote location, whether a gate in the airport or the distance to the city centre from the freeway. The time a traveller needs to reach a destination in airports and motorways depends as much on possible obstructions as on distance. Estimates of these two factors can best be quantified by stating how many minutes it takes to get there. No information is bad, distance given in metres is better, and information given in minutes on a static sign is probably still better. The best solution is a dynamic sign showing estimated time at the moment a traveller passes the sign.

Information about distance
Four options:

No indication
The traveller gets nervous: Will I be late for my connection or appointment?

Kilometres/metres
The traveller has no idea of obstructions: traffic, passport and security controls, accidents, toll booths, etc.

Minutes, static
Works fine with permanent traffic load.

Minutes, dynamic
Perfect.

Figure 96-97 Monitors are dynamic signs. Transport information. Seoul.

Figure 98 Descriptive sign. InfoWall, Metro. Copenhagen.

Figure 99 Descriptive sign. Canterbury Shaker Village, USA.

Figure 100 Descriptive sign transcending language barriers: E-R must mean Monday-Friday, and L and P Saturday and Sunday respectively. Tallinn, Estonia.

96
97
98

Sign functions
Regulation

All environmental signs are designed to influence the behaviour of those that read them. Otherwise they would have no function. Regulatory signs are more directly designed for this role than other signs. They bluntly tell readers the dos and the don'ts – what they must do and what they must refrain from doing.

Prohibitions are sometimes stated as warnings. A 'high voltage' sign, reinforced, with skull and crossbones exemplifies. The meaning remains the same: 'Don't touch'.

More than other types of signs, regulation signs call for authoritative design. Capital letters and conspicuous – but not fancy – colours are two traditional design parameters for stating authority by graphic means. At other times, steady light, blinking light, or some kind of sound may create the necessary attention and seriousness.

102

101

Figure 101-105 Signs play several roles concerning safety and security.

Figure 101 Canine regulation.

Figure 102 Escape route sign.

Figure 103-104 Warning signs. Santa Barbara, USA.

Figure 105 Unstable cliffs. Twelve Apostles. Great Ocean Road, Australia.

96 W>W

103

104

105

Sign contents

This chapter deals with four types of sign content. They are all SIGNS in their own right, and as SIGNS they are all symbols with conventional meanings. The four types of sign content are typography, pictograms, arrows, and guidelines.

Sign contents
Typography

Letters, words, sentences, and larger texts on signs should be easily legible and readable*. Their purpose is to be seen and read. Legibility is more important than fashion. This applies to typography on signs even more than it does to typography in books and other printed matter. The wayfinder often has only one bullet in the gun, one chance to read a sign. A driver on the freeway cannot stop or drive backwards. He may not even be able to reduce speed. Many signs must be read while the sign reader moves changing both distance and angle to the sign. This means that planners must emphasise the functional demands on typography. The more critical the circumstances under which the sign must be read, the more carefully the sign must be designed.

Simple typefaces are easier to read than complex typefaces. However, simplicity must not develop into an oversimplification that compromises the basic letter shapes. The typefaces used on signs should not be too different from the typefaces familiar to prospective readers. Typefaces with a clear distinction between letters, between numbers, and between letters and numbers are better for wayshowing than typefaces with less distinction.

Some typefaces use more space than others. In signage design, space economy is an important factor. That means that a narrow typeface may be preferred to a broad typeface. However, narrowness tends to affect the size of the counters, the openings in such letters as a, b, d, and e, which in turn influence legibility from acute angles. The usefulness of narrow typefaces may conflict with the need for counters that are not too small.

Ascender length and descender length also influence legibility. Too short ascenders and descenders reduce legibility. On the other hand, long ascenders and descenders occupy more vertical space. The optimal solution requires balancing the trade-off between these two elements.

Ordinary letter forms are generally better than italic and bold varieties. These are more difficult to read, and they should be reserved for special purposes.

*In daily parlance the words 'legible' and 'readable' are used interchangeably. In typography, however, legibility deals with type design while readability deals with the way the type is used.

Typography

Given the typeface, text written in sense case – normal orthography with upper and lower case – is more legible than text written with all caps – upper case letters. The ascenders and descenders of lower case letters make the largest difference between words, helping readers to read faster than they can read text written in all caps.

The fact that short texts such as 'STOP', 'HIGH VOLTAGE', or 'WARNING' are often written with all caps does not change this principle. The caps in these signs are chosen to emphasise authority.

For maximum legibility, letter spacing and word spacing – the horizontal distance between letters and words respectively – should be normal or slightly larger than on printed matter. When possible, letter spacing should be refined by kerning that alters the space between selected pairs of letters to make the text appear more balanced.

Line lengths should be moderate to support readability.

Line spacing – the vertical distance between text lines – should be generous to separate messages and support legibility.

Type size determines the distance at which letters can be read. A rule of thumb suggests calculating maximum reading distance as the multiple of x-height times 500. This rule of thumb means that a sign text with an x-height of one centimetre would have a maximum reading distance of five metres. In health care environments, signage planners should reduce the multiplier to 400 or even to 300.

106

Figure 106 Frutiger 69 Bold Condensed (top) is used in Oslo and Stockholm airports. Bembo Bold (below) was until recently the preferred typeface for signs in Heathrow Airport.

Departure

Frutiger 67
Bold Condensed

Departure

Info Medium

Departure

Info Semibold

Departure

Info Bold

Departure

Signa Condensed Bold

Departure

DIN Mittelschrift

Departure

Univers 67
Bold Condensed

107

Figure 107 This text with x-height 10 mm can be read by normal sighted people at a distance of 10mm x 500 = 5 metres.

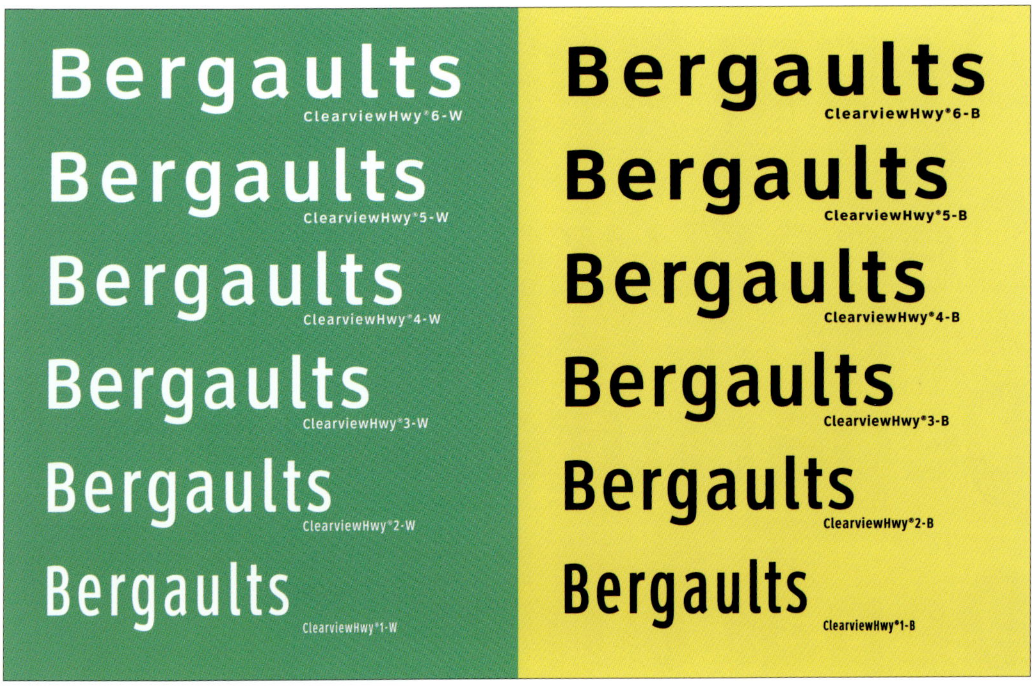

Typography

Figure 108 Clearview Hwy is the new typeface used for road signs in the United States. It replaces the FHWA typeface. While FHWA was designed for signs with capitalised words Clearview Hwy is designed for signs with mixed case (upper and lower case letters). Clearview Hwy is characterised by relatively large counters – openings in a, e, etc. – and by a relatively large x-height. Clearview Hwy is designed in six weights for use on dark and bright surfaces. Design Meeker & Associates.

Figure 109-110 Clearview Hwy has also been chosen for street signs in New York City. Mixed case will replace the old all caps signs.

Figure 111 Road sign with the old FHWA typeface.

Figure 112 Road sign with Clearview Hwy typeface. Compare the counters and the x-height with FHWA.

111
112

Typography

Text in the western world is normally written horizontally from left to right. This also applies to sign text. However, when space is scarce, especially on protruding signs, text may occasionally be written vertically. There are three different ways to do this.

First, letters may be placed horizontally under each other. As a rule, this should only be done with all caps and preferably only with short words.

Second, a text line may be turned 90 degrees to the right to be read from the top down. This can be done with all caps and – if necessary – with mixed case letters, but never with italic letters.

Third, a text may be turned 90 degrees to the left to be read from the bottom up. This is a bad idea. One reason is that we normally read top down. Another reason is that if something blocks the view of a part of the sign, this part is typically the lower part. This obstructs the beginning of the text. But this type of text messages can more easily be understood without the end than without the beginning.

113

Figure 113 In some quarters vertical signs seem to be the rule. Chinatown, New York.

Figure 114-125 Three kinds of vertical signs.

Figure 114-117 Short words, all caps, letters on top of each other to be read top down.

Figure 118-121 Letters turned 90 degrees to the right to be read top down.

Figure 122-125 Letters turned 90 degrees to the left to be read down up. A bad idea.

104 W>W

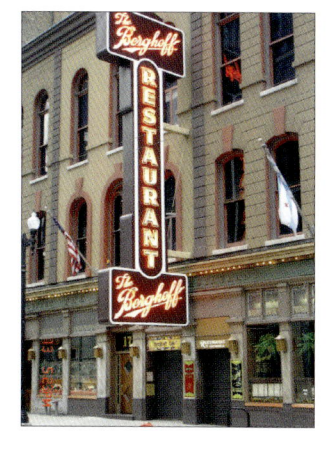

114
115
116
117

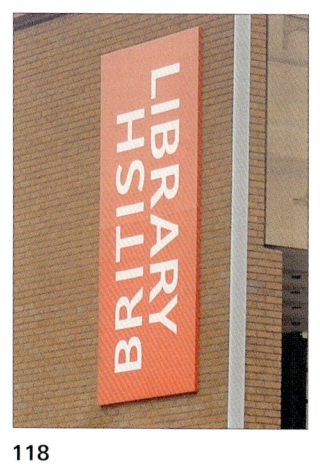

118
119
120
121

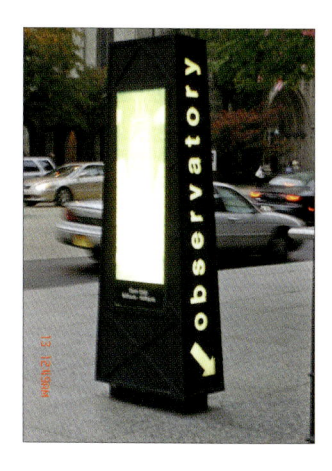

122
123
124
125

W>W 105

Sign contents
Pictograms

In principle, pictograms are pictorial signs that signify what they depict. As nonverbal signs, they are designed to help people with different language backgrounds as well as people with certain types of reading problems. In addition, pictograms should be faster to 'read' than corresponding text and thereby also help people who know and can read the relevant language.

The function of the pictogram requires both motivation and convention. First, pictograms should be highly motivated. They should depict a concept in a way that intended viewers immediately understand. Pictograms should be icons or, to be more precise, images. Second, pictograms should be standardised. They should be well publicised and used widely and consistently to teach intended users their meaning.

To the degree that a pictogram fails to meet one of the two conditions of motivation and convention, the other condition becomes more important. If a pictogram reader cannot see what a pictogram depicts, it is good to remember what it means. If the pictogram reader cannot remember having seen the pictogram before, it is good to see and understand what it depicts and thereby understand what it means.

Not all pictograms are sufficiently motivated or conventionalised. Not all pictograms are immediately understandable, and the standardisation of pictograms is less than ideal. On one hand, the pictogram pricing policy of ISO, the International Organization for Standardization, effectively keeps the ISO pictogram standard secret. It cannot even be seen on the WWW. On the other hand, several more or less private organisations sponsor their own standards.

Pictograms are ideograms, graphic symbols that represent an idea, object, function, or situation by visual likeness.

Pictograms that show the idea directly such as a picture of a train that represents a railway crossing, are motivated SIGNS, they are icons or images.

126
127
128

Figure 126-128 Toilet pictograms for Expo 98, Lisbon. Design Shigeo Fukuda.

Figure 129 AIGA pictograms. While the ISO standard is de facto kept secret, the pictogram series sponsored by AIGA, American Institute of Graphic Arts, is published for free use and in many ways functions as an international standard.

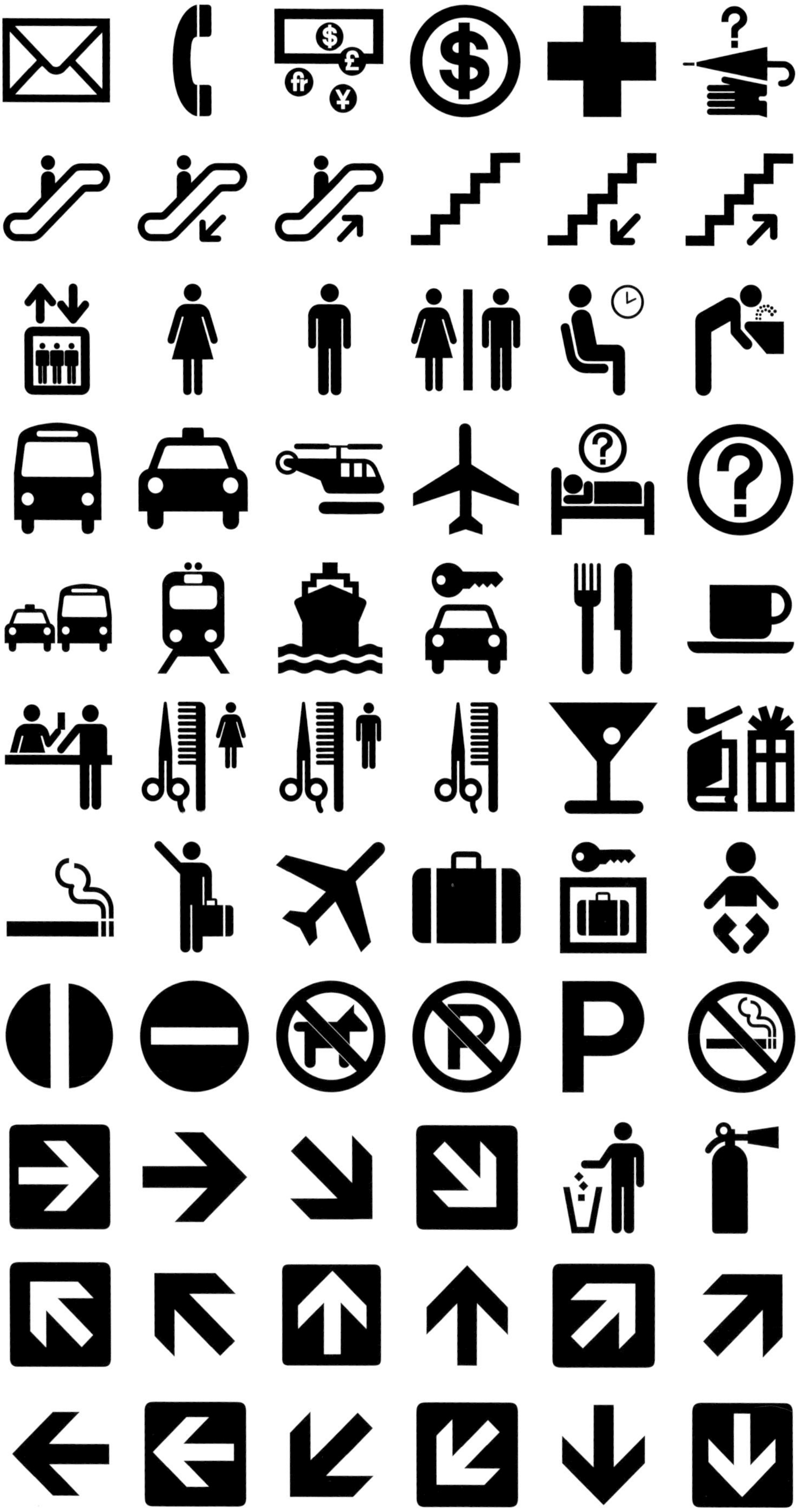

129

Pictograms

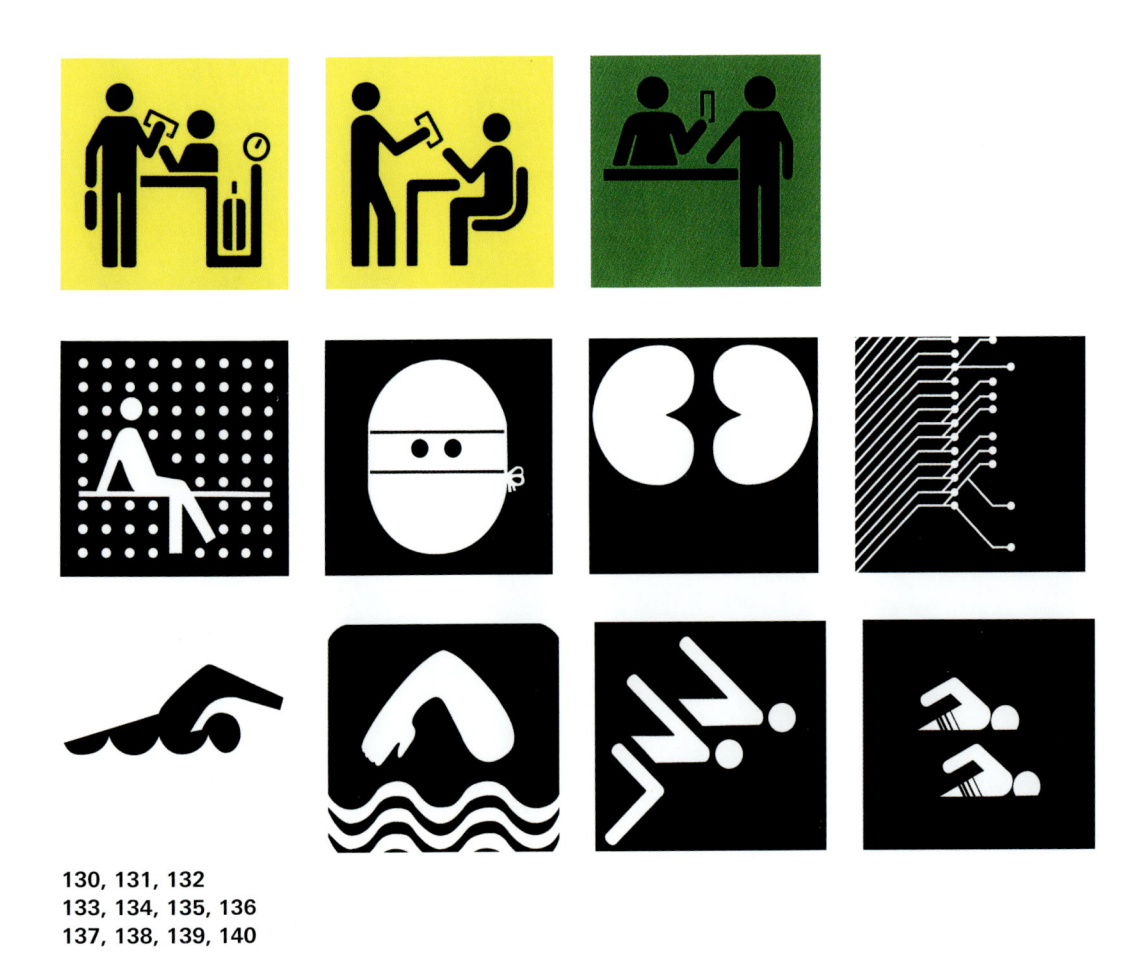

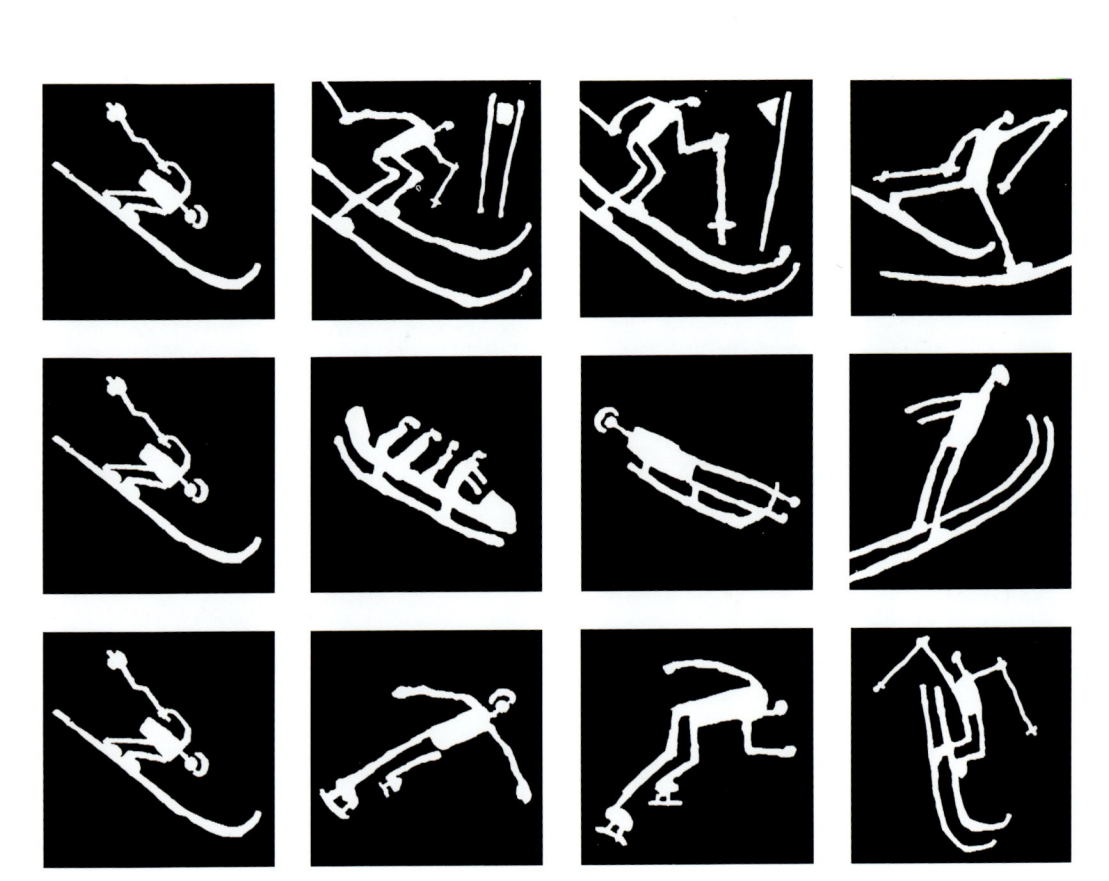

130, 131, 132
133, 134, 135, 136
137, 138, 139, 140

141

Pictograms that show the idea schematically, such as knife and fork (restaurant), are motivated SIGNS, they are icons or diagrams.

Finally, pictograms that show a concept schematically, such as a red circle crossed by a white bar, are arbitrary SIGNS, they are symbols.

Strictly speaking, SIGNS in the latter category are not pictograms, as they lack visual likeness. They are only understood because of convention. For practical reasons, however, we treat them as pictograms. After all, pictograms are conventionalised, and therefore they are symbols.

Pictograms may not be understandable for several reasons. Some situations are difficult to depict in a way that is immediately comprehensible to the intended readers. Many wayfinders with a different language background will also have a different cultural background. This may add to the difficulty of understanding pictograms. Toilet pictograms rarely depict exactly what they mean.

Pictogram designers occasionally seem to be more interested in artistic expression than in being understood by intended users. On other occasions, pictograms are poorly designed in terms of communication. What should be a solution becomes a new problem.

Many pictograms are not needed. Many others are wrongly conceived and not understandable. Some pictograms are decorative rather than informative. Some messages are better expressed with words than with pictograms. That was the assumption when the Charles de Gaulle airport in Paris was built. No pictograms were allowed in the aerodrome. All information on signs was given by text in French and English. Later, pictograms were introduced to the newer parts of the airport.

Figure 130 To mark every check-in counter in an airport with a pictogram showing a check-in counter that can easily be seen is signage abuse.

Figure 131-132 One of these two airport pictograms means transfer check-in. The other means ticket office.

Figure 133 The word 'sauna' seems to be universally understood. The pictogram is not.

Figure 134-136 Debatable hospital pictograms: Emergency Ward, Urology, Neurology.

Figure `137-141 Sports illustrated. Organisers of Olympic Games tend to consider pictograms an important part of their branding.

Figure 137-140 Swimming: Tokyo 1960, Mexico City 1968, Munich 1972, Seoul 1988.

Figure 141 The pictogram designers for the Olympic Winter Games in Lillehammer 1994 took their inspiration from a four thousand year old Norwegian rock carving with the world's oldest rendering of a skier. As with sports pictograms from other Olympic Games, one must be a true connoisseur to tell what is what.

Pictograms

142

Figure 142 Examples of pictograms designed by Otl Aicher and marketed by ERCO, the German specialist in architectural lighting. The collection is comprehensive.

Figure 143-144 The ERCO pictograms are a further development of the pictograms Aicher did for the 1972 Olympic Games in Munich.

Figure 145 Pictograms for Victoria and Albert Museum, London. Design Holmes Wood.

Figure 146 Pictograms for Virgin Atlantic, London. Design Holmes Wood.

143
144

145

146

W>W 111

Sign contents
Arrows and more

Graphic arrows are pictorial metaphors. Unmetaphorically, a drawing of an arrow is an image of standard ammunition from the time when bows were a major weapon for war and for hunting. The principle of metaphors is that we don't interpret the represented phenomena one-to-one, but detect the characteristics relevant in the actual context. In contemporary signs, an arrow is not coded and decoded to mean 'old fashioned lethal weapon'. The arrow is meant and understood to indicate the direction shown by its orientation.

Arrows are not the only graphic means for showing direction. A pointed hand – known in the printing business as a printer's fist – is used for the same purpose. Escape signs that show a running man (in Germany pursued by flames) are other directional SIGNS. Graphic footprints on the floor or ground also show direction. Finally, sometimes the direction of a sign can by itself show direction.

149
150

147
148

Figure 147 In Ephesus, Turkey, these two thousand year old footprints together with money (rectangles) showed strangers in this part of the Roman Empire the way to the bordello.

Figure 148 Russell Square, London.

Figure 149-150 Escape route signs.

Figure 151 Fifth Avenue, New York.

112 W>W

Empire
State
Building
PSYCHIC
READINGS
23W35ST
PALM
AROT CARDS
Advice On
All Problems
347-628-1091

151

Arrows and more

Figure 152 Sometimes the orientation of a sign makes arrows redundant. Tibirke, Denmark.

Figure 153 Santa Barbara, USA.

Figure 154 The location of the sign makes the sign understandable. Denmark.

Figure 155 Versatile pedestrian sign. Vienna.

Figure 156-157 Trondheim, Norway.

Figure 158 Australia.

Figure 159 Denmark.

Figure 160 Makepeace Woodcraft School, Parnham Dorset, UK. Design The Partners.

152
153
154
155

114 W>W

156
157
158
159

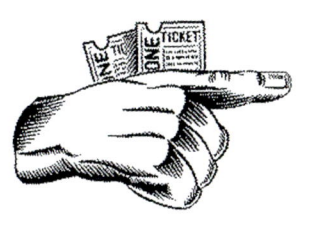

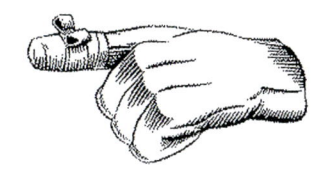

160

W>W 115

Arrows and more

161

162

163

Figure 161 School crossing. Vienna.

Figure 162 The arrows show where you should wait and then enter the train, and where you should not stand. Taipei.

Figure 163 Conflicting messages.

116 W>W

Sign contents
Guidelines

Guidelines can be a great help both to wayshowing staff and wayfinding patients in hospitals. Both wayshower and wayfinder can concentrate on one thing: follow the red line.

However simple, guidelines may be misinterpreted. Guidelines are in principle bidirectional. The red line on the floor that shows the way from the hospital front desk to the X-ray room also shows the way back. People with reduced learning skills may become confused about the direction and return to their point of departure.

More than one guideline in the same place may confuse wayfinders. When a hospital places other guidelines next to the guideline leading to the X-ray room, patients may mix them up and end in the wrong place.

Guidelines are also used at ferry harbours to tell automobile drivers where to wait and which way to enter the ferry. Sometimes lighting lines on the ground are used for that purpose.

164

165

Figure 164 Guidelines have many functions in public transportation. Taipei.

Figure 165 Guideline. Peter MacCallum Cancer Centre. Melbourne.

Sign form

The previous chapter dealt with content parameters. This chapter deals with form parameters: colour, size, shape, grids, and grouping. These are the wayshowing designer's command variables.

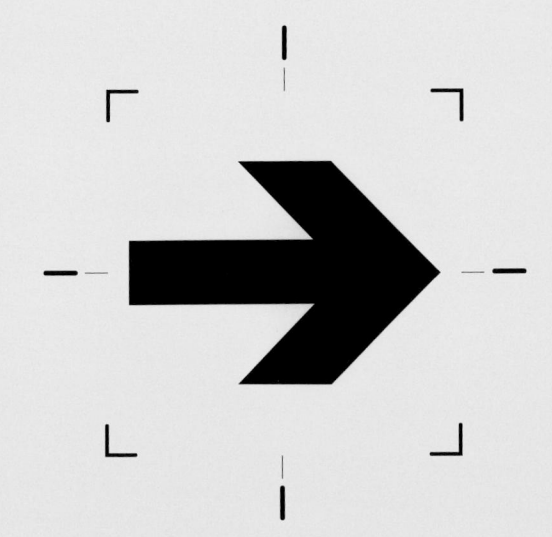

Sign form
Colour

Colour is instrumental to most kinds of visual signage. The physical fact is that graphic design is all about variation in colour on a surface. Colour can be seen from greater distance than other graphic elements. In signage, the primary role of colour is differentiation.

First, colour contrast between a signboard and its background gives the sign its target value, the ease with which the sign is spotted. To have practical value signs must be noticed. Many signs fail on this basic technical level. Outdoor background colours against which the signs should contrast are typically green plants, yellowish or brownish brick walls, and greyish concrete walls. Indoor background colours are typically white and fairly bright shades of other colours. Signs must be noticed against these backgrounds. If they are not noticed, they have no value.

Second, colour contrast between signboard and sign content makes the content readable. Sign content is letters and non-alphabetical symbols.

The first and the second issue merge into one issue when letters are painted or mounted directly on a wall or other background without an intermediate signboard.

Third, colour contrast between different signs may facilitate visual differentiation between different types of messages. We see this on motorways in countries where green signs refer to destinations on the motorway while blue signs refer to destinations outside the motorway system. In the same vein, some airports use different sign colours to differentiate signs related directly to traffic from other signs. In this way, colour may convey part of the sign's meaning before the content is read.

Fourth, colour contrast between different content elements within a sign may facilitate differentiating between different types of messages. On signs with bilingual texts, colour coding may help to distinguish one language from the other.

Colour

Colours play an important role in signage because of their capacity to differentiate. Signs require contrast between colours. However, colour contrast or colour difference involve more than one well-defined concept. The NCS Natural Colour System© helps us to understand colour contrast.

NCS Natural Colour System© is a colour description system based on six elementary colours: four chromatic and two non-chromatic colours. The four chromatic colours are yellow, red, blue, and green. The two non-chromatic colours are black and white. NCS describes the six elementary colours with respect to four visible qualities: hue, blackness, whiteness, and chromaticness.

The NCS is visualised by a three-dimensional model named the NCS Colour Space. It has the shape of a double cone. In principle all visible colours have a fixed position in the NCS Colour Space and a corresponding notation.

For better understanding, the NCS Colour Space can be divided into two two-dimensional models: the NCS Colour Circle and the NCS Colour Triangle.

The NCS Colour Circle is a horizontal section through the 'equator' of the NCS Colour Space where the four chromatic elementary colours are placed like the cardinal points in a compass.

Each quadrant between two elementary colours is divided into 100 equal steps. Every 10th step is shown in the NCS Colour Circle. The designation of the colours found in the NCS Colour Circle describes the hue. The designation B90G stands for bluish green with 10% blueness and 90% greenness.

The NCS Colour Triangle is a radiating vertical section through the NCS Colour Space related to a specific hue. The base of the triangle is the grey scale from white (W) to black (S). The apex of the triangle – coinciding with the Colour Circle – represents the maximum chromaticness of the current hue. Any specific NCS Colour Triangle shows all nuances of a hue.

In the NCS notation 1050-Y90R, 1050 describes the nuance, i.e. the degree of blackness, chromaticness, and whiteness. Whiteness, blackness, and chromaticness are stated as percentages with sum 100. In fact, only blackness and chromaticness are directly represented in NCS notations. Whiteness is given indirectly as the residual of 100 minus blackness and chromaticness. 1050 means 10% blackness and 50% chromaticness, leaving 40% whiteness.

In the NCS notation 1050-Y90R, Y90R describes the hue, in this case the degree of resemblance with yellow and red: 10% yellowness and 90% redness.

Pure grey colours – colours on the axis of the NCS Colour Space and on the base of the Colour Triangles – have no hue and are given nuance notations followed by –N to describe 'Neutral'. The pure grey scale goes from white to black. 90–N describes 90% blackness, 0% chromaticness, and 10% whiteness.

As a descriptive tool, the NCS allows designers to define three distinct types of colour contrast: contrast in hue, contrast in chromaticness, and contrast in brightness.

Contrast in hue is illustrated by the difference between colours occupying different positions on the NCS Colour Circle. The largest contrast in hue occurs between colours positioned opposite each other on the NCS Colour Circle. Colours in different NCS Colour triangles have different hues.

Contrast in chromaticness is illustrated by the distance between any colour and the grey (black/white) axis. The largest contrast in chromaticness is between a colour of the NCS Colour Circle and the black/white axis. Colours with different distance to the grey axis always have different levels of chromaticness.

Colour

Contrast in brightness is illustrated by the black/white axis. The largest contrast in brightness is between white and black. However, colours outside the black/white axis also possess some degree of brightness. This varies both with the content of black and white and with the hue. For instance, the elementary colour yellow is brighter than the elementary colour blue. Brightness in terms of luminous reflectance can be seen in the NCS Lightness Table.

When sighted people think of colour differences, they normally think of difference in hue: green, yellow, etc. For visually impaired people, however, colour brightness is a more relevant colour parameter. Wayfinders with visual impairments may find it easier to discern between bright blue and dark blue than to discern between a blue and a red of equal brightness. The most important colour contrast to people with impaired vision is contrast in brightness defined as colour reflectance. It is more important than difference in hue and contrast in chromaticness. Before choosing colours for signs, sign designers should evaluate the contrast in colour reflectance. ADAAG recommends a 70% difference in colour reflectance for a signboard and its background.

The NCS nomenclature is not generally used by industry. For ordering industrially painted surfaces, RAL is the relevant description system. For ordering vinyl lettering, sign planners use designations suggested by important suppliers such as ScotchcalTM/3MTM. For electronic displays, a hexadecimal colour system is commonly used.

Colours fade as time goes by. Some colours and some materials fade faster than others. Planners should ask suppliers for guarantees.

ADA
Americans with Disabilities Act

ADAAG
ADA Accessibility Guidelines

NCS
Natural Colour System©

RAL
A German colour specification system:
Reichs Ausschuss für Lieferbedingungen.

Learn more about the NCS – Natural Colour System© at www.ncscolour.com

Figure 166 The NCS Colour Space visualises the NCS Natural Colour System©. In principle, all visible colours have a fixed position in the Colour Space and a corresponding notation.

Figure 167 The NCS Colour Circle is a horizontal section through the 'equator' of the NCS Colour Space. All hues are represented her.

Figure 168 The NCS Colour Triangle is a radiating vertical section through the NCS Colour Space. The base of the triangle is the grey scale from white (W) to black (S). The apex of the triangle is the maximum chromaticness (C) of the current hue.

166

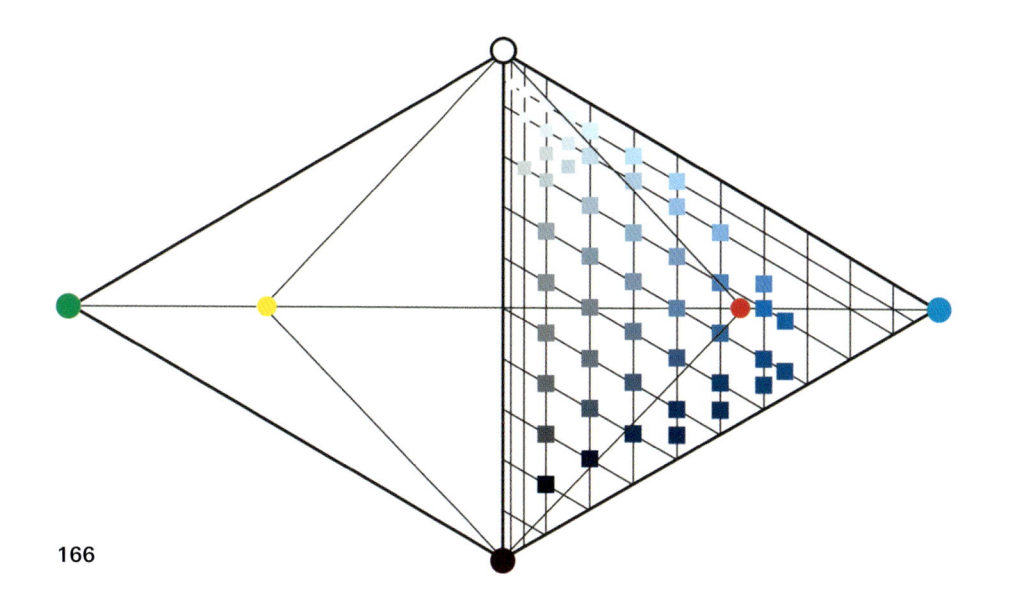

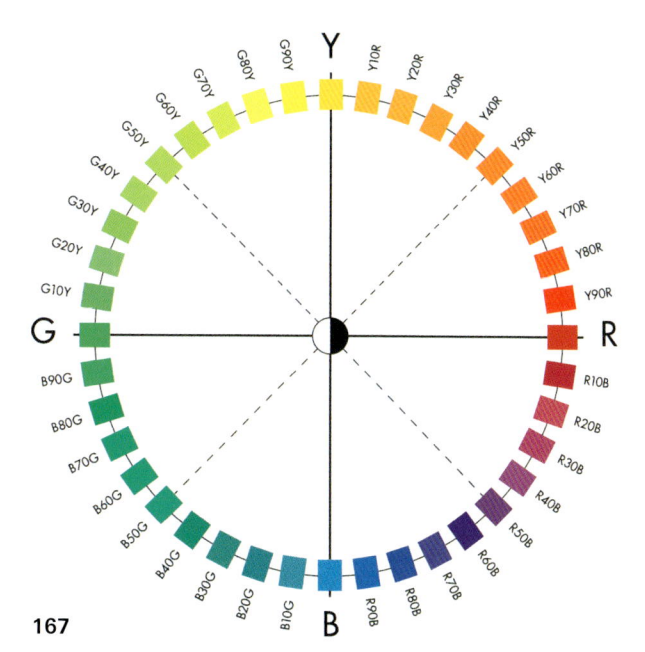

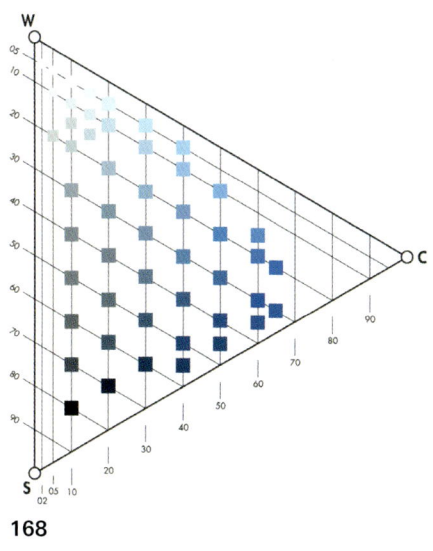

167

168

W>W 123

Colour

Glossy surfaces reduce legibility. Matte surfaces are more vulnerable to wear and more difficult to keep clean. The preferred solution is a reasonable trade-off between legibility and costs of maintenance. While gloss 60 (scale 0-100) may be a reasonable level on outdoor signs, gloss on indoor signs can go as low as 20.

It is a general assumption that a black figure on a yellow background provides the highest possible target value. It is easiest to spot. That is the reason why rescue material, civil work machinery, and warning signs often use these colours. However, there are situations where we refrain from this aggressive colour combination for practical and aesthetic reasons. Yellow and black together tend to create an atmosphere that easily is understood as 'danger'. Few airports want this. Passengers are already sufficiently motivated to look for the signs. It is generally wise to reserve yellow and black for situations where they are really needed.

Safety colours – such as the green colour used on escape signs – should not be used on other indoor wayshowing signs.

The problem of colour blindness should also be taken into consideration. *See page 149.*

Using colours from the company's corporate design program for wayshowing may be tempting, but this is not always a good idea. As a rule, company colours are not chosen with signage in mind, but sometimes they are. Identification signs with the corporate colours of major car rental firms serve as beacons: yellow/black = Hertz, red = Avis, green = Europcar, orange = Budget Rent a Car. Patrons of McDonald's and Pizza Hut know exactly what colours to spot in streetscapes to locate their preferred food.

Irrespective of wayshowing functions, the artistic use of colours may add to the aesthetic appearance of the environment. The practices identified in *W>W* present implicit evidence for this.

Colour coding different parts of a site can be a useful wayshowing device, but this should not be overdone. What looks good on the drawing board may function less effectively in reality. The more colours that planners use to emphasise messages, the less those colours will emphasise. Most people cannot effectively remember more than four or five colours.

On ferryboats where passengers leave their cars on one of two car decks, it can be a good idea to paint the decks in different colours and name them accordingly: Red Deck and Blue Deck. Some hospitals colour code various sections. To function as intended, such systems shouldn't have too many colours. All colours should be easily discernible, and they should have a name on which everybody agrees. Finally, colour coding systems should respect the needs of colour-blind users.

Figure 169 Colour on screens is a field of great interest. For JR Japan Railways Keiichi Koyama made a selection of six colours out of 16.7 million possible colours to eliminate the glare of the default settings.

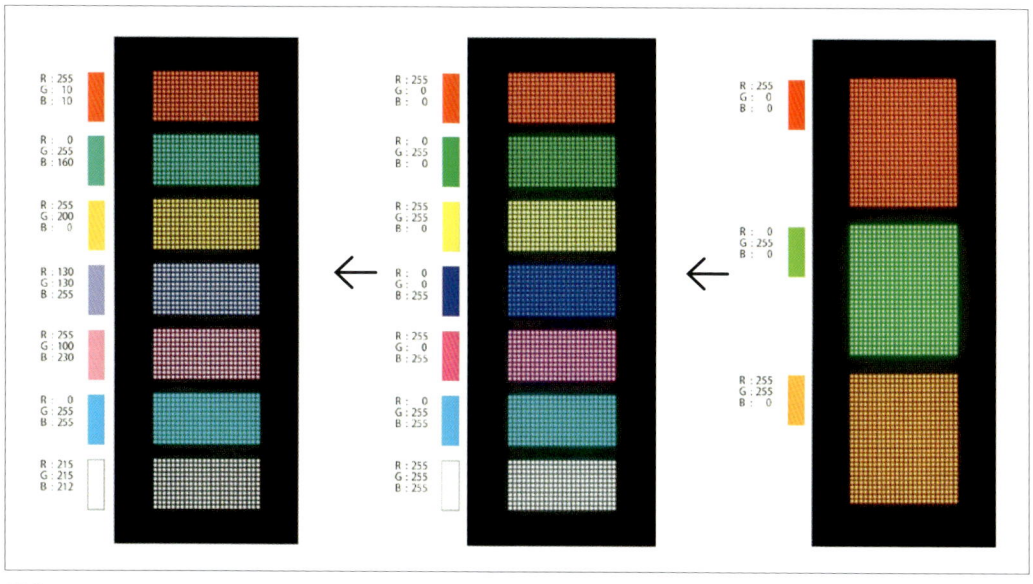

169

Colour

170

171
172

Figure 170 Colour contrast serves three purposes in these signs from St. Olavs Hospital in Trondheim, Norway. First, the colour of the signboards separates the signs from their surroundings. Second, the colour of the signboards separates permanent signage (blue) from temporary building site signage (orange). Third, the colour of the text and the arrows separate the sign content from the signboard. Design Mollerup Designlab & Frisk Architects.

Figure 171-172 Pragmatic colour coding. Male blue, female pink, children everything. Seoul.

Sign form
Size

Environmental signs must comply with three wayshowing functions. First, they should announce their own presence. They must have target value. Second, they should be easily readable. Sign size should give room for sufficiently large and readable content. Third, signs must, sometimes, show hierarchy: important signs should be larger than less important signs.

Size matters. Nevertheless, too large signs will damage environmental aesthetics and they will have an undesirable cost effect. Further, overly large signs are sometimes less visible than smaller signs. This is the case, for example when a large sign is situated outside the end of a narrow corridor. Only a fraction of the sign can be seen from the corridor. Finally, overly large signs may contribute to a feeling of information overload. Here, as elsewhere, the best solution is a trade-off between contrasting arguments.

173

Figure 173 More people may want to know the way to Stephansdom (St. Stephen's Cathedral) in Vienna than to the nearest fast food restaurant. Sign sizes sometimes create absurd hierarchies.

W>W 127

Sign form
Format

For most signs, the precise shape of the signboard does not play any role in the wayshowing function. However, a signboard may occasionally have a shape, which itself is a message. This is the case when the signboard has the shape of an arrow or a pointing hand.

In some countries, circular, triangular, and rectangular signboards give part of the meaning to road signs. Circular signs are used for commands, prohibitions, and restrictions. Triangular signs are used for warnings. Rectangular signs are used for general information. In the United States, triangular and circular signs are used to identify male and female toilets.

When it comes to sign systems for wayshowing it may be a good idea to determine the length of a signboard as a multiple of its height. This has practical and aesthetic value and will result in harmonising signboards and facilitate the grouping of signboards.

175
176

174

Figure 174 The shape of the arrow signs is itself a message. Santa Barbara, USA.

Figure 175-176 Triangular and circular signs used to identify male and female toilets. USA. Here with upper case and mixed case letters respectively.

Figure 177 In USA and many other countries, railroad crossings are marked with X-shaped signs. Santa Barbara, USA.

177

Sign form
Grids

Grids are systems of graphic guidelines that help to design signs that work together in systems. Grids assist the designer by setting standards for the distribution of content elements on a sign. In this way, these standards help to create results that harmonise with each other, turning plurality into unity.

In principle, grid-based signs can be designed in two ways, the build-up method and the breakdown method.

With the build-up method, the graphic designer begins with the message to be signposted and the necessary size of content elements. Applying the message and content elements to a universal grid with rules for margins will determine the format of the sign. The build-up method is typically used to design one-off signs.

With the breakdown method, the graphic designer begins with an eligible sign format with a format-specific grid and margins to see if it fits the necessary content. If the chosen sign format doesn't fit the intended content, the designer will try another standard format or try to adjust the content. The breakdown method is typically used for signs that are parts of sign systems.

Both universal and format-specific grids typically work vertically as well as horizontally.

Ideally, the vertical grid of a sign should be determined by the type size, which is itself determined by the minimum reading distance.*

For the relationship between type size and reading distance see page 100.

Vertical and horizontal grids are completed by rules for margins.

Figure 178 Format-specific grids used for interior directional signs, St. Olavs Hospital. Trondheim, Norway. Design Mollerup Designlab & Frisk Architects.

2.0 Henvisning
2.1 Innendørs henvisning
2.1.2 Mål (fortsatt)

← Poliklinikk øye
Kirurgisk intensiv og postoperativ
Poliklinikk øre / nese / hals

42 mm | 63 mm | 42 mm ... 42 mm
42 mm / 21 mm / 31,5 mm / 21 mm / 31,5 mm / 21 mm / 42 mm
840 x 210 mm

← Poliklinikk øye
Kirurgisk intensiv og postoperativ
Poliklinikk øre / nese / hals

60 mm | 90 mm | 60 mm ... 60 mm
60 mm / 30 mm / 45 mm / 30 mm / 45 mm / 30 mm / 60 mm
1200 x 300 mm

← Poliklinikk øye
Kirurgisk intensiv og postoperativ
Poliklinikk øre / nese / hals

84 mm | 126 mm | 84 mm ... 84 mm
84 mm / 42 mm / 63 mm / 42 mm / 63 mm / 42 mm / 84 mm
1680 x 420 mm

← Poliklinikk øye
Kirurgisk intensiv og posto
Poliklinikk øre / nese / ha

120 mm | 180 mm | 120 mm
120 mm / 60 mm / 90 mm / 60 mm / 90 mm / 60 mm / 120 mm
2400 x 600 mm

Eksempler på henvisningsskiltenes mål.

Skilt-bredde mm	Skilt-høyde mm	x-høyde mm	Lese-avstand m
840	210	21	6,3
1200	300	30	9
1680	420	42	12,6
2400	600	60	18

Sammenhengen mellom henvisningsskiltenes størrelse og leseavstanden.

Skiltmanual St. Olavs Hospital, Trondheim
Siden er opprettet / sist revidert 09 mai 2003
Mollerup Designlab A/S

19

Sign form
Grouping

Signs sometimes appear in unorganised clusters that blur impressions while hindering overview and fast orientation. Rules for grouping signs should be an integral part of any professional sign system. Signs can be grouped vertically, horizontally, or both.

Signs that are grouped vertically should preferably have equal width. Signs that are grouped horizontally should preferably have equal height.

In groups of signs with arrows, those with arrows pointing up should be placed at the top of the group, while signs with arrows pointing down should be at the bottom. Signs with arrows pointing to the left should be at the left side of the group, and signs with arrows pointing to the right should be at the right side.

Fingerpost signs are a special kind of sign group dedicated to directional signs. Each sign points in its own direction *(see page 93)*.

Figure 179 Vertical and horizontal grouping of signs. Oslo Airport. Design Mollerup Designlab.

Figure 180 Arrow positions on signs. Swedish airports. Design Mollerup Designlab.

179

180

Mise en scène

Signs are the carefully prepared actors of the wayshowing stage. Location, mounting, and lighting are the features of set design that help signs perform – or render them invisible. Location, mounting, and lighting are key factors. Planned well, nobody talks about signs; done wrong, they can spoil everything.

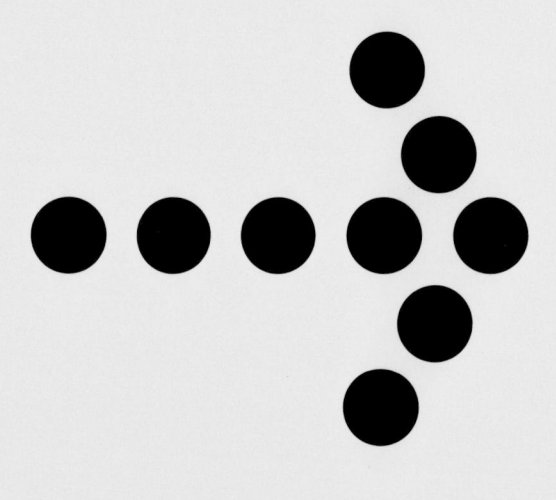

Mise en scène
Location

Signs should be located where they are needed. This truism is often neglected.

The basic double function of sign reading requires placing signs to be noticed and read:

First, a sign should be noticed and identified as a sign.

Second, a sign should be read and understood.

The second function implies the first. If we don't notice a sign, the fact that we – theoretically – can read it has no value. If, on the other hand, we notice a sign, we can often approach it to improve our reading conditions.

One important principle is not to provide wayfinders with information before they need it. Information given too early may confuse and be forgotten when needed. This is the principle of progressive disclosure.

Locating signs when needed involves at least four types of situation:

First, sign users need information at choice points, places where they must choose among alternatives:

– Should we continue along this avenue or turn left?

– Should we drive through the city or take the circular road?

Second, sign users need information when they are in new situations:

– Where am I?
– When is this clinic open?
– How do I use the emergency call point?
– Where are the rest rooms?

Location

Third, sign users need information when they are unsure or insecure:

– Has the last bus come yet?
– Am I following the right corridor? It seems very long.

Fourth, sign users need information when action will affect safety:

– Can I cross the tracks here?
– Is this road through the pass safe without snow chains?

When considering the location of a sign, the planner should take two issues into consideration. One is the distance from where the wayfinder will be when reading the sign*. The other is whether the wayfinder will be in motion when reading the sign.

For the relationship between type size and reading distance see page 100.

Three factors influence sign reading by moving sign readers:

– The reader's speed.
  The greater the speed, the more difficult the reading.
– The reader's distance from the sign.
  The longer the distance, the more difficult the reading. If a sign is very large, too short a distance can also be a problem.
– The reader's moving direction relative to the orientation of the sign.

Sideways signs offer more difficult reading than perpendicular signs.

These three factors are combined in the tables on the opposite page.

Mise en scène
Orientation

The most effective way to catch the attention of passersby is to locate signs perpendicular to their direction of movement. Important signs should preferably be oriented this way. Less important signs can be located along the direction of movement.

These rules comply with most people's intuitive wayfinding. When we look for important general information we expect to find it in front of us. When we look for less important special information we are prepared to look along the walls, or perhaps in the outskirts of the room or other areas. We have a similar experience in the supermarket. Soft drinks are placed more conspicuously than shoe polish.

In fairly large spaces, room signs and business signs can be mounted flat as a rule. In narrow spaces such as corridors and narrow streets, room signs and business signs can be protruding to allow observation from a distance.

Signs on fingerposts should point in appropriate directions.

Figure 181-182 Use these tables as a point of departure for your own considerations.

Sign location and readability			
Reader's speed	Distance to sign	Sign orientation	Ease of reading
high	short	perpendicular	OK
high	short	sideways	very difficult
high	long	perpendicular	easy
high	long	sideways	OK
low	short	perpendicular	very easy
low	short	sideways	easy
low	long	perpendicular	very easy
low	long	sideways	easy

181

Wayfinder characteristics				
	Speed	Can slow down	Can stop	Can go back
Motorists	high	sometimes	sometimes	no
Cyclists	medium	yes	yes	sometimes
Pedestrians	slow	yes	yes	yes

182

Mise en scène
Height

Average eye height is a reasonable starting point for positioning signs that sign users must read while standing or walking. However, other practical factors often make it reasonable to position signs above average eye height.

People, vehicles, and other objects easily block signs with relatively low positions. A position above eye height will allow more people to study the sign at the same time. When 400 or more people leave a large aircraft, only the first ten will be able to see a sign at eye height at any one time. The next passengers will see nothing until the first passengers move on.

The importance of a position above eye height increases with the distance from which a sign should be seen. To be seen from a fairly long distance, signs must be placed at a height of between 210 and 240 centimetres – possibly higher, depending on the situation.

As a rule, room signs at doors should be positioned on the wall next to the knob or handle side of the door, generally with a top height of about 170 centimetres. At important doors that many people use, larger signs can sometimes be positioned over the door to provide greater visibility at a distance. Signs should preferably not be placed directly on doors. They cannot be seen when the doors are open.

Wheelchair-bound wayfinders prefer signs in fairly low positions.

Figure 183-184 Protruding and suspended signs must be mounted with sufficient leeway to avoid collisions.

Figure 185 Flat mounted signs must be mounted in a certain height if they shall be seen from a distance or by many people at the same time.

Figure 186 Freestanding signs are easy to see, but may be problematic with respect to people with poor sight, and to good traffic flow and cleaning.

Figure 187 Door signs and flat mounted signs that shall not be seen from a distance or by many people at the same time can be positioned at eye level.

240 cm   240 cm   240 cm

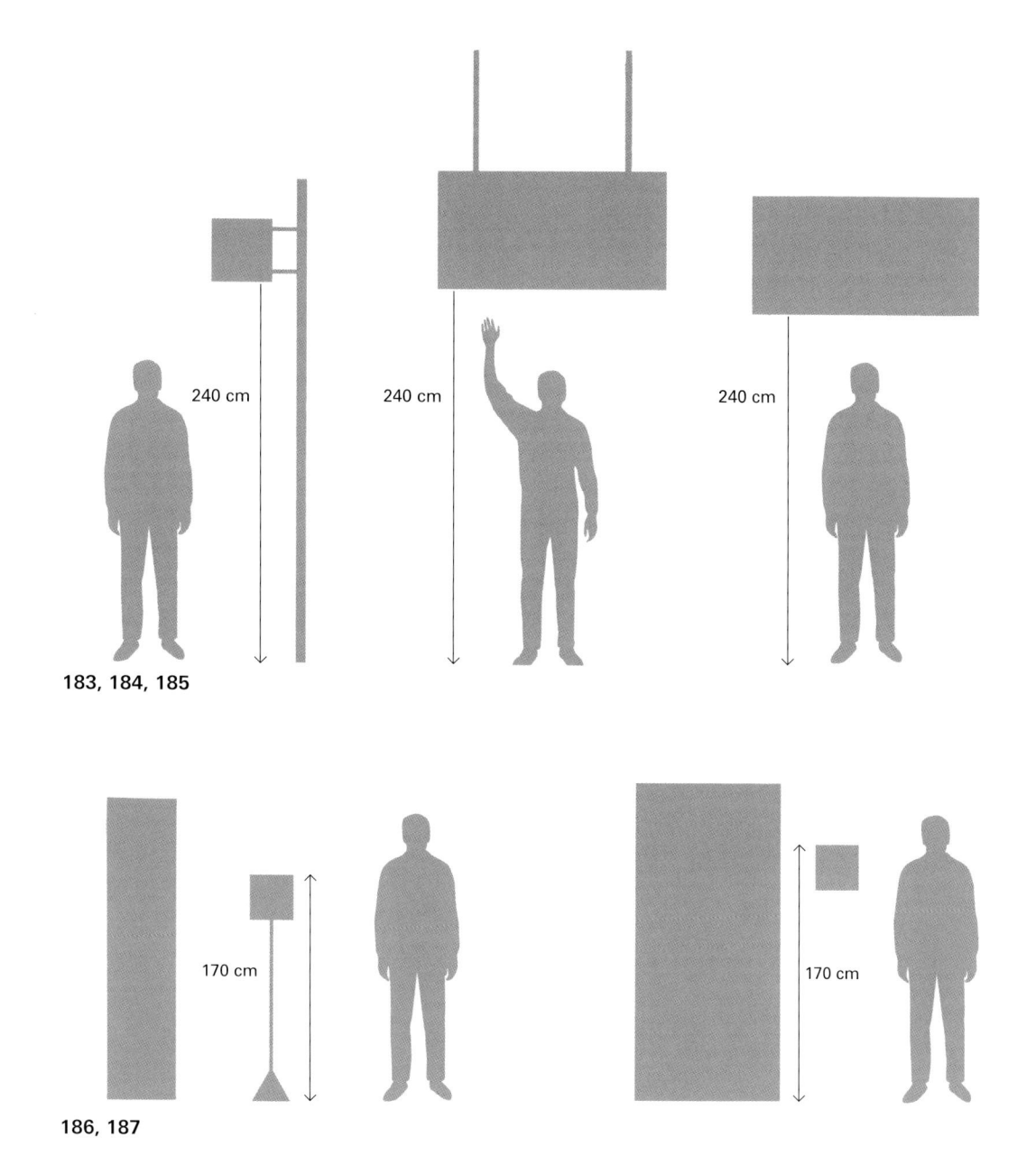

183, 184, 185

170 cm   170 cm

186, 187

W>W 139

Mise en scène
Mounting

Signs can be mounted in several ways, each with usability characteristics, advantages, and limitations. Apart from airborne signs, all methods can be used indoors as well as outdoors. For obvious reasons, airborne signs are restricted to outdoor use.

	Indoors	Outdoors
Flat mounted	x	x
Protruding	x	x
Suspended	x	x
Freestanding	x	x
On the floor/ground	x	x
In the air	–	x

Flat mounting is the most common type of mounting. Flat mounted signs are one-sided signs. Room signs located at doors are a subcategory of flat mounted signs.

Protruding signs are two-sided signs with a message on one or both sides. They are most often used in corridors and narrow streets where – in contrast to flat mounted signs – they can be seen from a distance. Protruding signs must be positioned at a certain height to permit free passage under the sign.

Suspended signs are two-sided with a message on one or two sides. Suspended signs are good for large indoor areas when placed at appropriate height for long distance viewing and with appropriate leeway and appropriate orientation. The portal is a special version of the suspended sign, a signboard suspended between two pylons.

Freestanding signs are debatable. Their virtue is that they can be located exactly where planners want them. Their flaw is that they may be obstructions to visually impaired people, cleaners, and others. Freestanding signs can have one, two, or more sides. They can be slabs, pylons, or columns, or they can be fingerposts.

Floor-signs are interesting. Perhaps the first wayshowing sign in the world was a sign on the ground, possibly a broken branch, or a scratch in the ground. Most environmental signs are positioned at or above eye height. This is convenient for most users most of the time. However, there are times when signs placed on the ground may offer an alternative solution to an important wayfinding problem.

One reason for placing signs on the ground may be that this is the last resort. If walls are not available, if there is no nearby ceiling from which signs can be suspended, and if there is no space for freestanding signs, then floor-signs may be considered.

The needs of blind people and people with poor sight offer another reason for floor-signs. To people with poor sight, graphic information on the ground may offer the best possible distance for spotting and reading. To blind people, tactile patterns on the ground may offer useful guidance.

Figure 188 Traditional floor-sign. Lisbon.

Figure 189 Floor-sign. Kansai International Airport, Japan.

Mounting

Outdoor signs on the ground have limited value in areas where the ground may be covered with snow or dirt. Even then, outdoor signs on the ground are already common in traffic. Striped pedestrian crossings address pedestrians who should use them and drivers who should respect them. Motorists and bikers follow lane stripes. Sometimes they read text and arrows on the ground, and they may respect full stop lines.

In concourses and other indoor environments, static or dynamic signs may be projected on the floor. Normally, this type of signage is only used for advertising, possibly due to its lack of authority.

Airborne signs identifying roadside restaurants may have some merit. They can be seen from long distance and they are easy to spot, since there are fewer objects competing for visual attention in the air. This argument may be weaker in built environments.

The long-distance effect of signs in the air depends on the height combined with the size of the sign. The higher the sign, the greater the distance to the viewer. At greater distances, signs should be larger and they should have sharper colour contrast. At greater heights, signs are more sensitive to weather conditions for visibility.

Signs in the air may serve as landmarks for fairs and various types of roadside business. Balloons reportedly boost turnover at fast food restaurants by large two-digit percentages.

Figure 190 The street sign cheers up pedestrians in the snow free part of the year. Seattle.

Figure 191 This ground sign suffers from bicycle parking. MuseumsQuartier, Vienna.

Figure 192 Cyclists beware of cyclists. Paris.

190
191
192

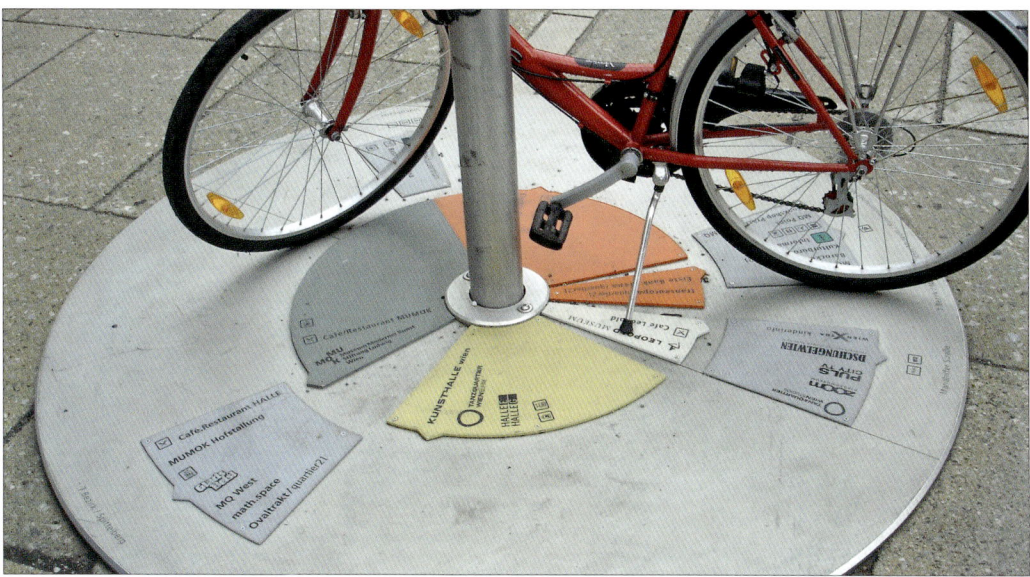

W>W 143

Mise en scène
Lighting

Signs should normally be seen. To be seen, signs must be lit externally or internally, or the sign content must be light itself.

Externally, signs can be lit indirectly by environmental light, or directly by spots.

Internally, fluorescent tubes or filament bulbs can light signs from behind.

Finally, signs can have lighting content. That is the case for signs where letters and non-alphabetical symbols are made of diodes or other light emitting units. This is also the case for neon signs.

ADAAG recommends that signboards should be given a light level of 70 lumen.

ADA specifies the illumination level on sign surfaces to be on the 100 to 300 lux range with uniform distribution over the sign surface. Other light around the sign should not significantly exceed the illumination on the surface.

ADA
Americans with Disabilities Act

ADAAG
ADA Accessibility Guidelines

Lumen
Unit for measuring the flux of light by a light source or received on a surface.

Lux
Unit for measuring the illumination of a surface. One lux is defined as an illumination of one lumen per square metre.

193

Figure 193-194 The medium is the message. Seattle.

Figure 195 Signs with lighting content. Centre Pompidou, Paris.

144 W>W

194
195

W>W 145

Signposting for visually impaired users

People with impaired vision or other physical or cognitive impairments require more from signs than other people do. They have a greater need for signs because they don't see, read, or move in the environment as well as others do.

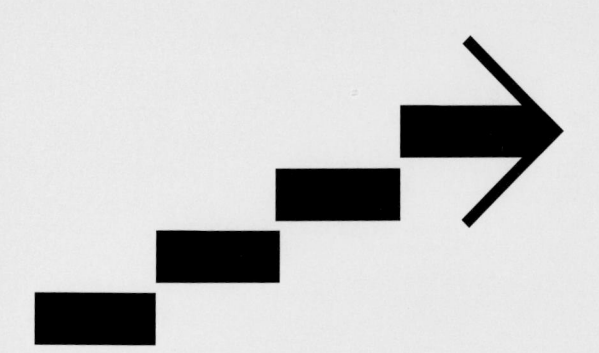

Signposting for visually impaired users
Inclusive vs. exclusive design

Sign planners can deal with signage for people with visual and other impairments in two ways. They can provide special wayshowing aids for impaired people, or they can make all wayshowing aids so good that they serve all people – with and without impairments. The first method is called exclusive design or the micro method. The second method is called inclusive design or the macro method. It neither excludes nor segregates potential users.

The exclusive solution with separate signs for sighted and visually impaired users means more signs, violating the basic principle of having as few signs as possible.

Another argument against the exclusive method – not generally accepted – is that it is less helpful for people with visual impairments to become used to special signs in protective areas in hospitals and other health care institutions when the world outside can't be improved.

The best possible solution is probably a robust inclusive method reinforced with some extras for visually impaired people.

Some of the efforts that benefit people with visual and other impairments also benefit – or at least don't handicap – people without impairments. All users prefer signs of good size with clear typography, good colour contrast, and no glare. Other improvements for visually impaired users, such as Braille, are hardly noticed by users with normal sight.

Sighted people may see other adjustments for visually impaired users as quality reductions. This is the case for some signs placed at eye height that allow readers to go as near as they want. These signs allow close-readers to block the view for other people.

The following sections discuss wayshowing means for the visually impaired. These include signposting. Visual impairment is more than one thing. A short introduction to different types of visual impairment will suggest the difficulty of making effective signage for everybody at the same time.

Inclusive vs. exclusive design

← Poliklinikk øye

← Poliklinikk øye
Kirurgisk intensiv og postoperativ
Poliklinikk øre / nese / hals

→ Kirurgisk intensiv og postoperativ
Poliklinikk øye

↘ Poliklinikk øye

↓ Kirurgisk intensiv og postoperativ
Poliklinikk øye

196

Signposting for visually impaired users
Visual impairments

Visual impairments can roughly be sorted into two broad classes. Loss of general sharp vision is one. Loss of vision in particular areas is the other.

Loss of general sharp vision covers a continuum of dysfunctional sight. This begins with a slightly blurred picture that becomes increasingly blurred and indistinct before ending with totally blurred vision.

Loss of vision in particular areas includes central field loss, peripheral field loss, and a combination of these two impairments. Central field loss means that visually impaired people cannot see what they look directly at. They can only see what happens at the periphery of the visual field. Peripheral field loss is sometimes referred to as tunnel view. That means than only the centre of the visual field is seen.

Colour blindness covers a wide range of difficulties of seeing colours. It is thought that 6% of the male population and 2% of the female population suffer from some kind of colour blindness, a genetic inability to distinguish differences in hue. Only a very few colour-blind people can't see colours at all. Most colour-blind people suffer from difficulties discerning red from green. They can't become aviators, but they can still get a driver's license. They need the sign designer's support.

Figure 196 Inclusive design at St. Olavs Hospital, Trondheim, Norway. Clear colour difference between white walls, dark blue sign boards, and white letters and arrows, never more than three lines in one group. All arrows are near the beginning of the text – for the benefit of sign readers with loss of vision in particular areas. Design Mollerup Designlab & Frisk Architects.

Signposting for visually impaired users
Means

Environment
The physical design of the environment can involve several measures to help visually impaired wayfinders. First, the environment can be planned for consistency. Ladies' rest rooms can be located next to the men's rest rooms. Rest rooms can be located in the same place on all floors in the office building. Lifts can be situated next to the staircase. Things can be situated where they are expected to be.

Other measures include ensuring that walking areas are free of obstacles that hinder free passage. Differentiated flooring can help mark routes, for example the passage from one area into another. Clear differences in colour between floors and walls and doors help the visually impaired to orient themselves in locations they don't know.

Visually impaired people can benefit from sounds and smells that sighted people can also notice – but usually don't. Architects can influence the sounds of a room by specifying floor and wall materials.

Colour
Different visual impairments mean different capacities for discerning colour. Many visually impaired people can more easily distinguish between colours of different brightness than colours of different hue. A red and a blue of equal brightness can be much more difficult to discern than two red colours of different brightness.

Typography and language on signs
Typography and language that help visually impaired involve the same basic typography and language that help sighted people. This includes such factors as listed in the margin.

Factors that increase legibility and readability

- clear, simple typefaces
- no fancy typefaces
- good type size
- good letter spacing
- good word spacing
- good line spacing
- short lines
- short words
- generally known words
- short messages
- no fancy layout
- contents without gaps
- arrows placed close to the text they belong to

Braille

Braille is a system of SIGNS that can be read by touch using the hand. Braille SIGNS consist of one to six raised dots in a 2x3 matrix. That gives the system 63 possible SIGNS. Braille is not scaled up and down. There is no international standard concerning the size of the dots or their internal distance. In the United States, the following dimensions are specified by law: dot diameter: 0.059 inches, inter-dot spacing: 0.090 inches, horizontal separation between cells: 0.241 inches, vertical separation between cells: 0.395 inches. Braille is used in two different ways:

Grade 1 Braille. Each letter in the alphabet is represented by one SIGN. The SIGNS that stand for letters a to j also serve as numbers one to ten, but are preceded by a special SIGN (dots 3, 4, 5, 6).

Grade 2 Braille. Each SIGN stands for a common expression.

As a rule, simple words are spelled with Grade 1, while longer messages are written with Grade 2. For use on signs only Grade 1 is recommended.

One problem with Braille is that few people use it effectively. Denmark, for example, has roughly 1,000 fluent Braille users in a population of 5 million persons. Learning Braille implies both discerning between different SIGNS and knowing their meaning.

Another problem is that Braille cannot advertise itself at a distance. It has low target value. Braille signboards often come with a semi-circular locator, which helps users to feel the exact position of the SIGNS when the signboard is already found. Braille should be used in places where blind people who read Braille expect to find it, and when possible, they should be informed where to feel for it.

Further, Braille messages must be situated in certain positions, heights, and angles that allow users to touch and read them upside up with the hand in the correct position. Users in wheelchairs must also be considered.

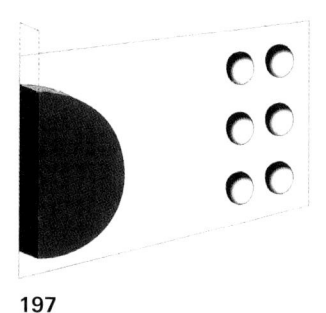

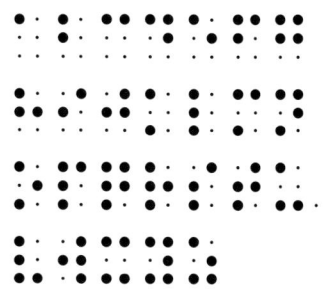

197

a/1 b/2 c/3 d/4 e/5 f/6 g/7
h/8 i/9 j/0 k l m n
o p q r s t u
v w x y z
198

Figure 197 Braille locator height 6 mm, width 3 mm, dept 1.5 mm.

Figure 198 Braille with Danish measures.

Tactile letters

People who have lost their sight may find reading tactile (raised) letters easier than to learn Braille because they already know the shape of the letters. Sighted people can also read tactile letter SIGNS if they have a colour contrasting with the background.

However, the use of tactile letters is limited by certain demands of the shape, size, and location. For easy 'reading', tactile letters should preferably be caps only. The height should preferably be between 15 and 50 millimetres. Letters should be raised minimum 2 millimetres and have rounded front edges. Like signs with Braille, signs with tactile letters must be placed to allow users to reach and 'read' them upside up with the hand in the right position. Users in wheelchairs must also be considered; the sign location for wheelchair users is not optimal for other people.

Tactile maps

Tactile maps are maps with all signatures raised to allow hand reading. These maps are problematic. While sighted people read the map and compare with visual surroundings, visually impaired people lack the important second part of that process. Sighted people can also benefit from tactile maps; they are informative and occasionally easier to read than flat maps.

Practical reasons limit the height of tactile maps. Users in wheelchairs must also be considered.

Figure 199 Tactile transportation map with Braille text. Copenhagen.

København 1978

Farum
Nærum
Holte
Ør Ra
Vr
Br
Fv Klampenborg
Sor Ll
Væ
Ly Jæ
Ha Sb St Or
Ba Gen Ch
Ki Ber
Bu
Vg Helle
Dg
Ballerup Em
Sko Her S
Ry
Hu No
Is Nb
Fu
Jy Van Go
Fre Np
Vest
Pb Kø
La Eng
Rø
Gl Bø Hvi Va Sy
Ab Ei Sj
Am
Av Fh
Vl Bs
Ih

199

W>W 153

Means

Practicalities

Visually impaired people prefer visible flat mounted signs at eye level. This allows them to approach the signs for close reading. Signs at eye level are not always a good solution for sighted people, especially not when signs must be seen at a distance by many people.

Suspended signs and protruding signs must have sufficient leeway to avoid collisions. The height makes it more difficult for the visually impaired to spot and read them.

Freestanding signs are obstacles to be avoided whenever possible.

Some visually impaired people prefer signs on the floor. This is obviously a problematic solution. Objects may be placed on the signs and other people can stand on the signs. Moreover, the signs will be worn down if they are not made of highly resistant materials. Outdoor 'floor-signs' may be covered by dirt and snow.

Signs to be felt – signs with Braille or tactile SIGNS – should be placed relatively low if they also address users in wheelchairs. The one-sign-fits-all approach implies a certain degree of compromise.

Talking signs or loudspeaker messages are highly desirable to people with visual impairments. Talking signs should always be used as supplements to visual signage. Sighted people also benefit from talking signs, especially at stations, and in trains, busses, and lifts.

Tactile guidelines on the ground help visually impaired people with or without mobility sticks to find their way at railway stations and other public environments. Such guidelines can be a great help for visually impaired without reducing the wayfinding quality for other people.

Figure 200-201 Pictoform wayshowing system for visually impaired pedestrians. The system includes tiles with raised lines and dotted areas as well as loose raised elements to be mounted in existing surfaces. Tiles come in cast iron and concrete, while loose elements are available in bronze and stainless steel. Design Knud Holscher & Charlotte Skibsted.

200
201

Interactive wayshowing

Interactive wayshowing is wayshowing enabled by devices that respond with wayshowing information when addressed by the wayfinder. Interactive wayshowing is also known as digital wayshowing (which also comprises non-interactive dynamic signs of many kinds). Interactive wayshowing devices include computers, kiosks, and handheld devices.

Interactive wayshowing
A digital friend

The best way to find one's way in terra incognita is simply to walk out there, read the environment, make decisions, and move: search, decision, motion. However, not all environments allow this. Wayfinders need help. The second best way to find one's way is to take advice from a friend who knows the territory. The friend should be available whenever help is needed. Such good friends are not in great supply. However, interactive wayshowing aids are digital friends that are always available, and they only offer advice when consulted.

The digital aids available at the beginning of the 2010s cover a spectrum of wayfinder needs, off-route and on-route, stationary and portable, strictly wayshowing, and enhanced with placeshowing.

These digital devices are fairly new and have not yet reached their final form. It is safe to predict that the future will bring devices that are easier to deal with, offering more and better advice than the solutions available today.

Interactive wayshowing
WWW

The role of the World Wide Web in wayshowing is primarily to assist off-location initial planning. While travellers are still at home, the WWW makes finding locations, venues, routes, and traffic connections far easier.

An important wayshowing function where the WWW is at its best is providing pre-visit information for venues such as airports and hospitals. Modern airports have several parking facilities with different distances from the terminals, and with different price levels, and length-of-stay specifications. Getting information about this and how to get from parking space to terminal buildings is much better done at home before the journey than at the airport a short time before departure. Wayfinding favours the prepared traveller. Large hospitals may be as complex as airports. Public transportation, parking spaces, and location of entrances and departments are all issues of interest to prospective patients, visitors, and others. These should be explained on the hospital website.

Computers come in portable versions. Many are still too clumsy for the physical part of the wayfinding process. On the other hand, using the stationary computer at home allows the traveller to print the necessary maps and other information retrieved, which may be more handy than a portable computer.

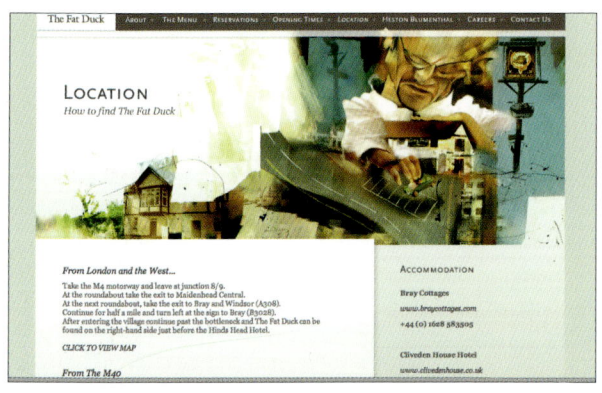

202

Figure 202 A first time visit to The Fat Duck restaurant in Bray, UK, or any other attraction typically starts on the WWW, which provides maps and driving directions.

Interactive wayshowing
Kiosks

Wayshowing kiosks are customised computer terminals located where needed in the environment, typically in foot traffic areas. These kiosks offer both wayshowing information and directory service: whereness and whatness.

Kiosks have been around for several years and have gradually developed from standard computer terminals with limited functionality to highly specialised devices.

One weakness of kiosks is that they can only be used by one person at at time. Another weakness – which may increase the effects of the first weakness – is that the typical user is a beginner. In fact, those travellers who are most in need of the kiosk tend to be novices. Still another kiosk weakness is that the user must remember the information given if the kiosk is not connected to a printer.

The development of large touch screens such as used by the New York's MTA, Metropolitan Transportation Authority, will probably characterise future kiosks. See page 192.

For kiosks compared with apps, see page 162.

Figure 203 New York subway touch screen kiosk. MTA.

203

W>W 159

Interactive wayshowing
Smartphone apps

Apps cover a wide field of wayshowing functions. They are basically of two kinds: general maps like Google Maps and location specific apps like the Kew Gardens app *(see page 222)*.

The various map apps available include simple scalable maps, maps with location of the user, and maps with route descriptions and oral assistance.

Most location specific wayshowing apps deal as much with placeshowing as with wayshowing. Whatness and whereness. Placeshowing often precedes wayshowing. For example, users of the (New York) Central Park app don't try to find the way to the Dancing Crane Cafe before they know of it.

To the target venue, a smartphone app means introduction of a degree of self-service as well as branding the venue as technologically advanced. Visitors with the relevant app will do much of their own wayfinding without troubling staff. Apps are applied experience economy with possibilities for advertising served as on-demand information.

Developing and continually updating a comprehensive app involves significant costs for the target venue.

To the visitor of a venue, a smartphone app means that he has all the necessary information, updated, interactive, and handheld. To some visitors an app makes wayfinding an entertaining game, a kind of treasure hunt.

On the other hand, the visitor must use the time necessary to download and repeatedly update apps. Also, the visitor may feel locked to the smartphone, watching the phone more than the environment. Some wayfinders need separate glasses for looking at the app on the smartphone and looking at the environment, accentuating this feeling. Further acquisition of route following information may hinder the creation of a robust cognitive map.

App = application software for mobile devices

Smartphone wayshowing and placeshowing apps: Benefits and burdens

Venue benefits
– Self-service
– Branding
– Experience economy
– Hidden advertising

Venue burdens
– Initial costs
– Updating costs

Visitor benefits
– Portable information
– Often updated
– Treasure hunt

Visitor burdens
– Download takes time
– Updating takes time
– Must be watched all the time
– Hinders studying the environment
– Hinders creation of cognitive map
– Small type may demand use of two pairs of glasses

Figure 204 Google Maps app.

Figure 205 Google Earth app.

Figure 206-209 Walk Brighton, UK, app. Home, attractions, shopping, nightlife. Map design AIG Applied Information Group.

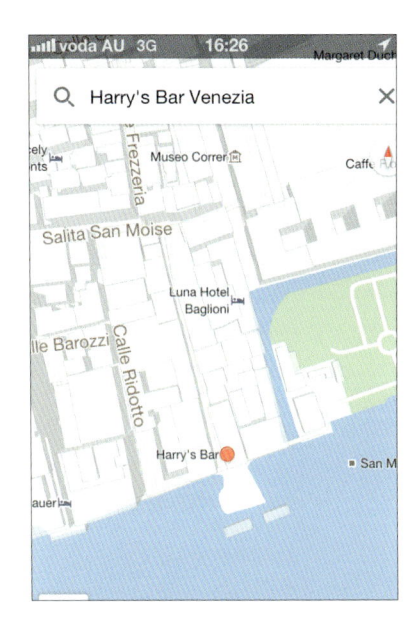

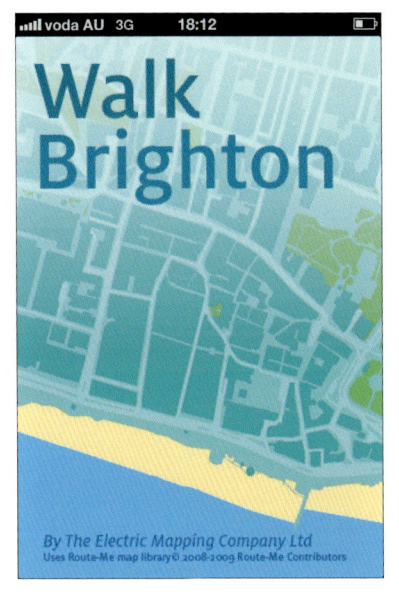

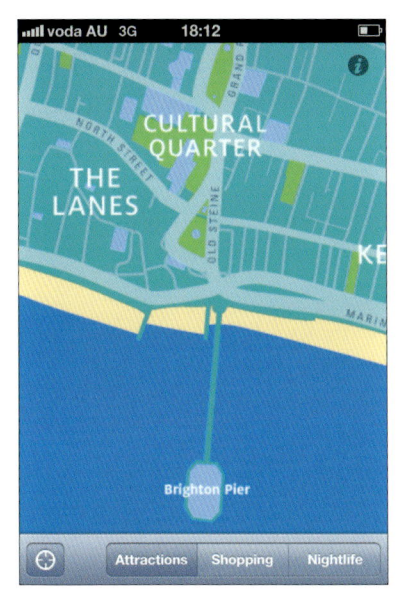

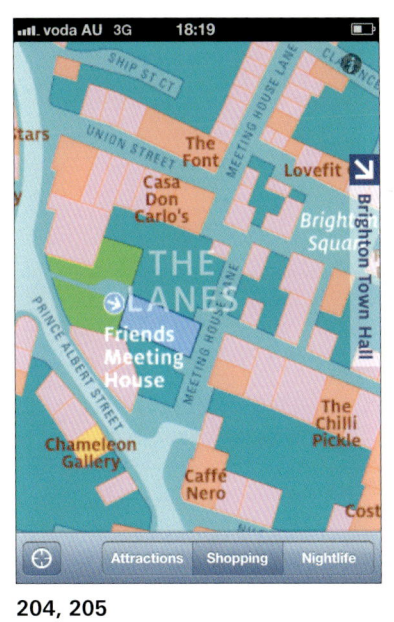

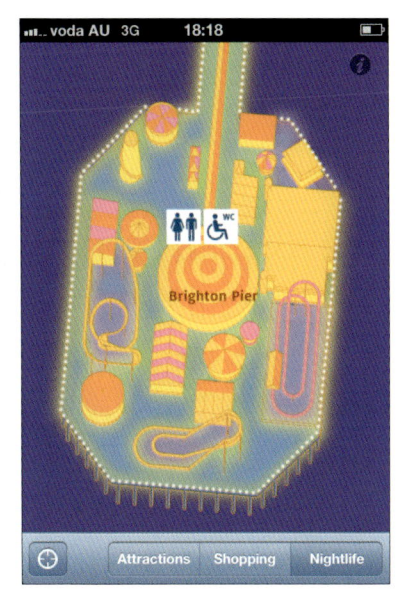

204, 205
206, 207
208, 209

W>W 161

Smartphone apps

Maps are the core ingredient of most wayshowing apps. The map typically has a zoom function and a you-are-here function. Arrows at the map edges may point to off-map destinations. Maps may have symbols for all kinds of attractions and service functions.

Touching a map symbol may call up a picture of that phenomenon and another touch may show the route from the present location. Some apps allow the user to customise the map by including or excluding categories of map symbols, such as museums and playgrounds.

Directories may have only one level or they may be hierarchical lists of places, functions, and other phenomena. Lists may be organised according to location or alphabetically. Selecting an item in the directory may lead to a map with the item positioned, which again may lead to a route description.

Some venues may choose between kiosks and apps and consider some of the following factors:

Apps	Kiosks
– can be used at home	– can only be used in situ
– exclusive: for some	– inclusive: for all
– reception problems?	– no reception problems
– steep learning curve	– flat learning curve
– everywhere	– only at certain positions
– no queue	– queues
– no wear and tear	– wear and tear
– no vandalism	– vandalism
– no outdoor problems	– outdoor problems
– low startup costs	– high startup costs
– small screen	– large screen
– no sound?	– sound?
– user update	– venue update
– works outdoors	– problems outdoors?

Wayshowing and placeshowing functions

Maps
– Zoom
– You-are-here
– Pointing to off-map destinations
– Showing places
– Showing directions
– Showing locations from directory
– Customisation

Directories
– Hierarchical lists of content organised by location or alphabetical
– Showing location on map
– Showing routes

Events
Calendar

Figure 210-211 Central Park, New York, app.

Figure 212-213 American Museum of Natural History, New York, app. Design Spotlight Mobile.

Figure 214-215 Federation Square, Melbourne, app.

162　W>W

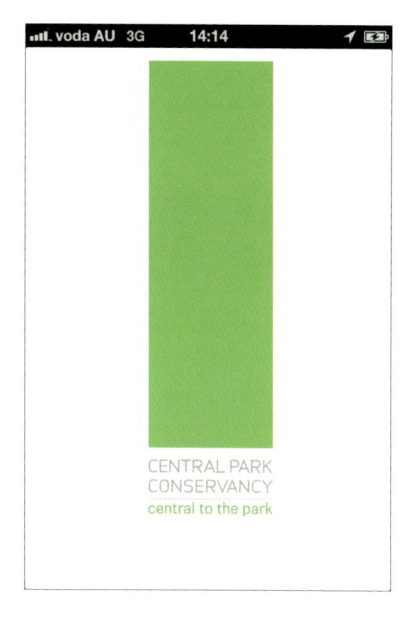

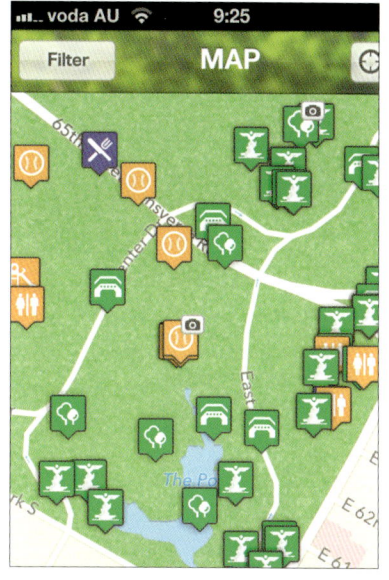

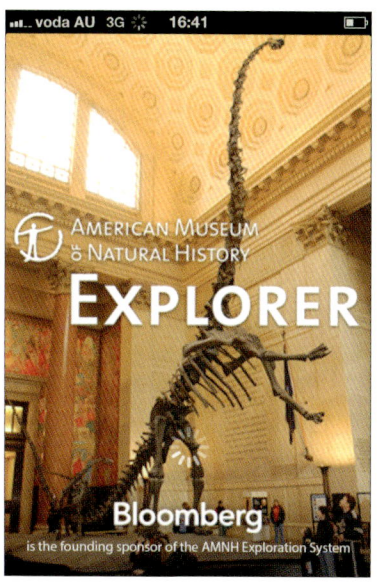

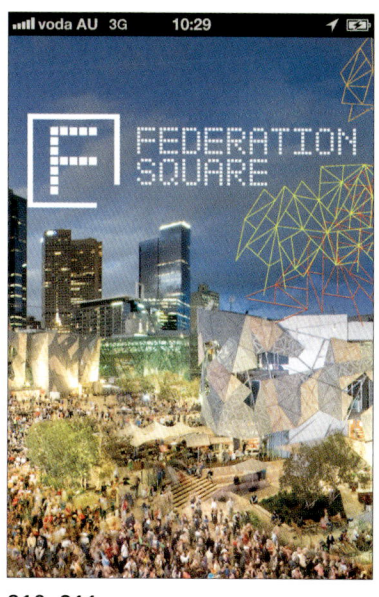

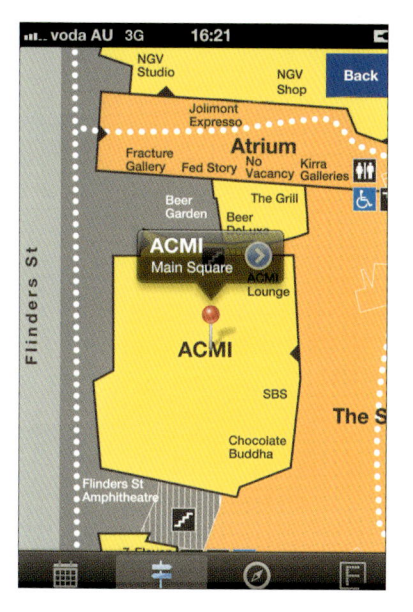

210, 211
212, 213
214, 215

W>W 163

Interactive wayshowing
QR codes

QR codes are two-dimensional scanner-read codes with storage capacities larger than standard UPC barcodes. The QR code was invented by Toyota in the 1990s to track automobiles through the manufacturing process. The code was originally patented, but is now made available free. Today, QR code is used intensively in advertising and packaging, but it also has the potential for wayshowing, particularly for placeshowing. Smartphone owners can download QR readers and simple QR code generators for free.

QR codes give venues an effective way to pass information to the receivers' smartphone. A URL given by the QR code allows the receiver to jump to the sender's website right on the smartphone. Using QR codes for wayshowing, and particularly for placeshowing, implies that the information doesn't occupy much space in the sender's venue and does not overwhelm uninterested travellers. Another advantage is that the traveller can keep the given information on his smartphone. Japan Railways use QR codes for transportation information (see page 190). Museums use QR codes for enhanced information about exhibits.

The capacity of a QR code depends on the kind of information presented: numeric, alphanumeric, byte or binary, or Kanji (Japanese writing system). A QR code can contain 4,296 alphanumeric characters. If a URL is used this limit is of no relevance.

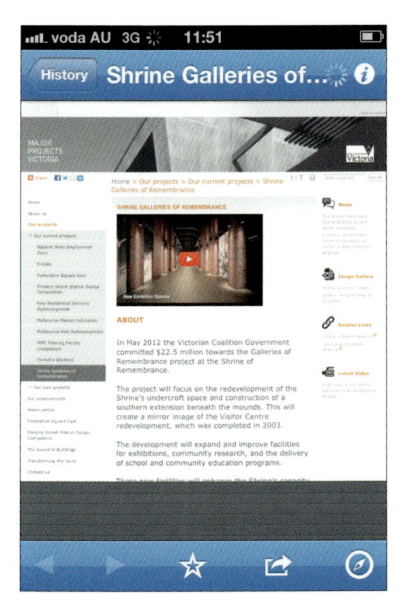

QR = Quick Response
UPC = Universal Product Code

216
217

218

Figure 216-217 Information board with QR code (at the bottom). The Shrine of Remembrance. Melbourne.

Figure 218 The QR code in figure 217 read by a QR scanner on an iPhone.

164 W>W

Interactive wayshowing
AR, Augmented Reality

As the name implies, Augmented Reality adds something to the real world. It happens by the use of a smartphone, tablet, or wearable internet ready device such as Google Glass with a – free downloadable – Augmented Reality browser. When the AR app is open, the camera on the device is activated, and the user will not only see what is in front of him, but also added information. The added information relates to things that are nearby.

What extras the user sees depends on position, direction, and choice from a menu: 'around me', accomodations, mountain peaks, or something else.

219, 220
221

Figure 219-221 AR seen on an iPhone.

Figure 219-220 AR in 'public space' showing customised attractions, restaurants, or something else, chosen from a menu. Works indoors and outdoors. Frederiksberg and Asserbo, Denmark.

Figure 221 AR in 'private space'. Here used to identify plants. Kew Gardens. UK.

W>W 165

Planning

Coordinated wayshowing doesn't simply happen. It is the result of a structured planning process. This chapter discusses the need for structured planning and outlines the elements of the planning process. The chapter concludes with a review of the issues of wayshowing that may involve corporate branding.

Planning
The need for planning

Good wayshowing adds to the function and value of an environment. It should be an integral part of general site planning. To plan wayshowing in a large building or any other area – built or natural – is a problem solving process. It should include all steps needed to move from a present state to a preferred state, from a state with little or no wayshowing to a state with improved wayshowing.

If architects and other planners neglect these issues, downstream planners will later need to solve the problems that architects and other planners leave behind. In the worst case, wayshowing design becomes repair design for architectural neglect.

Several wayswhowing measures are available to planners:

On-site	– Architectural and environmental features including circulation, transparency, and distinction
	– Landmarks
	– Toponomy
	– Signage
	– Information counters
Off-site	– Pre-visit information

The five on-site measures should preferably be planned in one coordinated process.

Pre-visit information on how to reach the site can be relevant to targets of any size. Pre-visit information on how to get around at the site should be relevant only exceptionally to such complex sites as large hospitals and airports.

Planning
The planning process

The planning process can be represented in a model with ten steps. Some steps can be subdivided. Other steps may not be distinct. They blend into each other and planners must deal with them more or less simultaneously.

The order of the steps indicates a logical sequence. Feedback should be included whenever appropriate.

Steps
1. Defining the problem
2. Setting the team
3. Seeking information
4. Analysing data
5. Developing a wayshowing strategy
6. Planning signage
7. Designing graphics
8. Designing hardware
9. Implementing the plan
10. Evaluating results

This overall list is a skeleton that can serve as a point of departure for several different kinds of planning processes. Much can be added; nothing should be taken away.

Step 1 — Defining the problem

Action
Start planning the wayshowing system by defining the problem.
If the problem cannot be described in full immediately, the description must be completed as soon as possible.
As in other problem solving processes, a good problem description will often point to the solution.

Questions
What is the real problem?
Are there related problems?
What is specific to this case?
When must the wayshowing system be ready for use?
What are the economic conditions?

Outcome
A problem description that serves as a job assignment for planners.

Well begun is half done.

Step 2 — Setting the team

Action
When the problem is defined, choose an appropriate team.
Those in charge must decide who is going to plan and who is going to decide on the wayshowing system.
Careful planning at this point will prevent time consuming discussions later.
Physical planning should be left to a professional wayshowing firm. The firm should refer to a steering group with representatives of building owners, architects, and users. The leading representative of the building owners will preside, see that the necessary decisions are made, and – if necessary – get approval at higher levels.

Questions
Does the team include the necessary qualifications?
Is the team too large to be operational?
What is the decision process?
Who can decide what?
Who is responsible for escape signage?
Is the team available when needed?

Outcome
A description of the wayshowing organisation with decision competencies.

The planning process

Step 3 Seeking information

Action Use the problem description developed in step 1 as a starting point for comprehensive information gathering. Consult building owners, architects, and users to determine all relevant information on the future state and use of the building.

Questions How – exactly – will the site be developed?
What is the intended circulation?
From where to where will most wayfinders move?
Who will use the site?
Will special groups of users need special attention?
Do user groups include people with special language requirements?
Will some users have mental, visual, or other disabilities?
When will users use the site?
Are monotonous building patterns seasoned with landmarks?
To what degree should corporate branding influence wayshowing aids?
Must other commercial considerations be accounted for?
Do tenants have special requirements?
What are the security requirements?
What kind of permits do public authorities require?
What names are to be used for places and functions?
Which similar sites should be inspected for inspiration and benchmarking?

Outcome Description of all issues that will influence wayshowing.

Step 4 Analysing data

Action Examine the information gathered in step 3 for wayfinding implications. Step 4 will sometimes overlap step 3 and step 5.

Questions How will intended users read the environment?
Will special kinds of audiences meet problems in wayfinding?
What times and places are most likely to create problems?
What are the critical situations?
Are suggested names for places and functions adequate?
Are names and numbers consistent?
Are names descriptive when possible?
Can intended users understand the names?
Is wayshowing in one language enough?
What are the success criteria?

Outcome A task description focused on functional requirements and possible problem areas.
Feedback on names (optional).

Step 5   Developing a wayshowing strategy

Action   Develop a comprehensive wayshowing strategy to describe how to meet every requirement clarified by step 4. The strategy should specify which wayshowing media will serve which requirements.

Questions   What role should pre-visit information play?
Can marking signs make directional signs superfluous?
Will y-a-h maps be helpful?
Will directories be helpful?
Will information kiosks be needed?
Are information desks with live staff necessary?
Are dynamic signs or monitors necessary?
Should there be a help desk that can be reached by port phones or mobile phones?
Does planning cover all groups with special needs?
Do architects and other planners need feedback?
Should interactive media be used?

Outcome   Wayshowing strategy.
List of requirements for pre-visit information.
Feedback for architects and other site planners.

Step 6   Planning signage

Action   Specify messages, graphic and physical sign types, and sign positions based on the wayshowing strategy.

Questions   What messages are needed?
Where are the messages needed?
What type of sign will suit these messages?
How should the signs be dimensioned, positioned, mounted, and lit?
What about ad hoc signage?
What should dynamic signs and monitors be programmed to do?
What role sgould interactive wayshowing have?

Outcome   Initial sign plans that serve as starting point for graphic and physical design and programming dynamic signs and monitors.

The planning process

Step 7 Designing graphics

Action Design graphic signs as specified in step 6.

Questions How many types of graphic sign design are needed?
What basic elements are needed?
    Typeface?
    Arrows?
    Pictograms?
    Colours?
    Other?
What formats and grids are needed?
What signware is recommended?
    Silk screening?
    Vinyl?
    Other?
What gloss is recommended?
What about dynamic signs, monitors, and kiosks?

Outcome Design specifications of all graphic sign types documented in a digital sign manual.

Step 8 Designing hardware

Action Design hardware of signs as specified in step 6.

Questions How many types of hardware sign design are needed?
What types of mounting are needed?
Does signage require standard hardware or customised hardware?
What about lighting?
    Environmental?
    External?
    Internal?
    Lighting sign content?
What about dynamic signs and monitors?
What about kiosks?
What about ad hoc signs?

Outcome Hardware design of all sign types documented in a digital sign manual.
Models of all hardware types.

Step 9 Implementing the plan

Action
Specification
Schedule
Requisition of quotes
Choice of suppliers
Ordering
Controlling
Claiming
Mounting
Controlling
Adjusting

Questions What can go wrong?

Outcome Fully signposted site.

Step 10 Evaluating results

Action
Evaluate the wayshowing after a period of use.
The evaluation has two purposes:
First, mistakes and omissions should be detected and corrected.
Second, the company should learn from past action to improve future performance.

Questions
Are there complaints or other indications of dysfunctional wayshowing?
How does involved staff evaluate the wayshowing?
How many visitors ask to find their way?
Should there be a user test?

Outcome Evaluation report.

Planning
Branding considerations

Today, most organisations plan site signage with a view to corporate branding and design programs. Site signage can influence an organisation's branding. Quite obviously, the company's wayshowing says something about the company's general capacity to deal intelligently with practical problems and about its care for people. Companies that lack interest and ability to provide decent wayshowing don't deserve respect and patronage.

Site signage is part of an organisation's body language. It sends continuous messages about the organisation's skills and attitudes. As a result, on-site signage contributes substantially to organisational branding. In contrast, while visitors are not forced to see the company's video presentation, or to read the image brochure, they must look at company signage to find their way.

Some organisations take the branding aspect of site signage quite seriously, often in sensible ways without forgetting the wayshowing considerations. Others tend to sacrifice the primary function of wayshowing signs on the altar of branding.

222

Figure 222 Branding and wayshowing. Melbourne.

Figure 223-224 The border between wayshowing, decoration, and branding is sometimes non-existent: adidas research and development building: adidas Laces, Herzogenaurach, Germany. Design büro uebele.

223
224

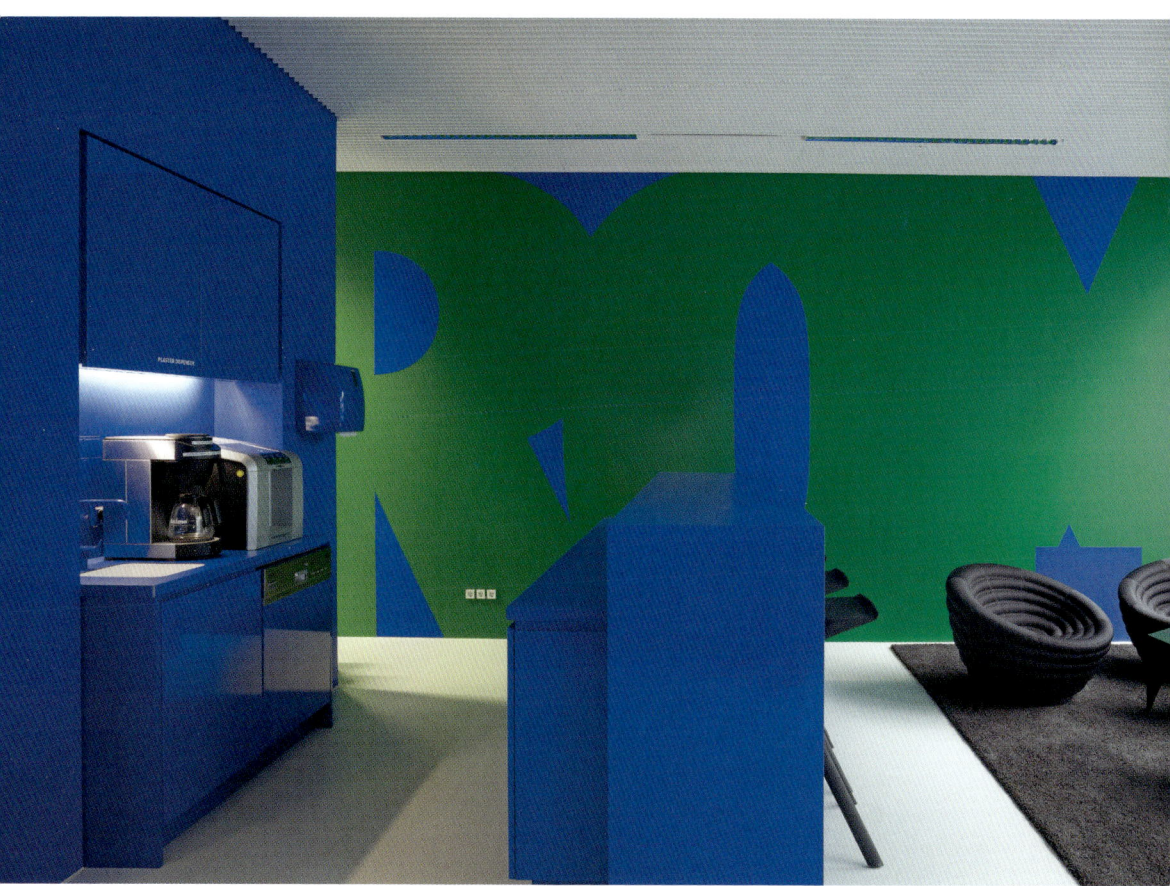

Practices

This part of *W>W* deals with the moment of truth: principles used in practice. The examples are organised in six categories:

– Airport
– Rail
– City
– Knowledge
– Culture
– Outdoor

>

Practices
Cases in point

The principles suggested in the first part of *W>W* are essentially normative. Through the power of argument, the book proposes some standards. This second part is purely descriptive, it uses cases to describe what several skilled practitioners of wayshowing have accomplished.

In addition to their professional qualities, these examples are selected to illustrate a broad variety of wayshowing solutions to wayfinding problems. The chosen cases are shown for understanding and reflection, rather than as examples for emulation.

It is not possible to fully demonstrate the qualities of wayshowing systems in a book. Many dimensions of excellent wayshowing systems can only be fully understood on location. Any representation of wayshowing systems is necessarily fragmentary, and they often suggest feeling rather than complete comprehension. However, our goal in presenting the wayshowing systems in this second part of *W>W* is understanding.

There are substantial differences between wayfinding problems in different environments. Appropriate wayshowing solutions therefore differ as well. Finding the way in metro systems and other urban transportation systems depends primarily on understanding the network; the problem is situated outside the station. Finding the way in airports is primarily transfer-related from ground transport to air transport, from air transport to ground transport, and from air transport to other air transport. Here the problem resides inside the airport. In other sites, wayshowing tends to deal more with placeshowing, whatness rather than whereness.

Airport
Berlin Brandenburg Airport

Berlin's new single airport in Schönefeld, south of central Berlin, will replace three airports in Berlin: Tempelhof Airport (closed in 2008), Tegel Airport, and the terminals of the existing Berlin Schönefeld Airport. The new airport is designed to serve 30–50 million passengers.

The wayshowing system of the airport creates a strong sense of place. The primary sign colour, red, is a reference to Berlin and Brandenburg. A secondary colour, dark grey is used for service information. In addition to the use of colour, line patterns emulating the style of the architecture and the landscape add to the identity.

The signage programme continues outside the terminal including traffic signs, signs in the parking garages, and signs for pedestrians.

The airport will open for traffic in 2014.

Design 2013
Architecture:
GMB Gerkan, Marg and Partners
Wayshowing:
Moniteurs

Figure 225-228 Berlin Brandenburg Airport.

225

226
227
228

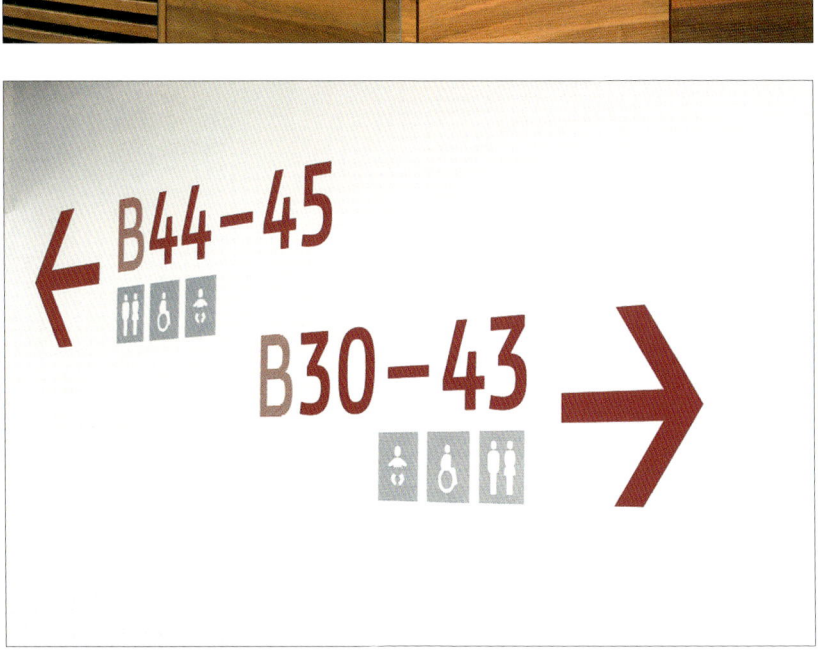

Berlin Brandenburg Airport

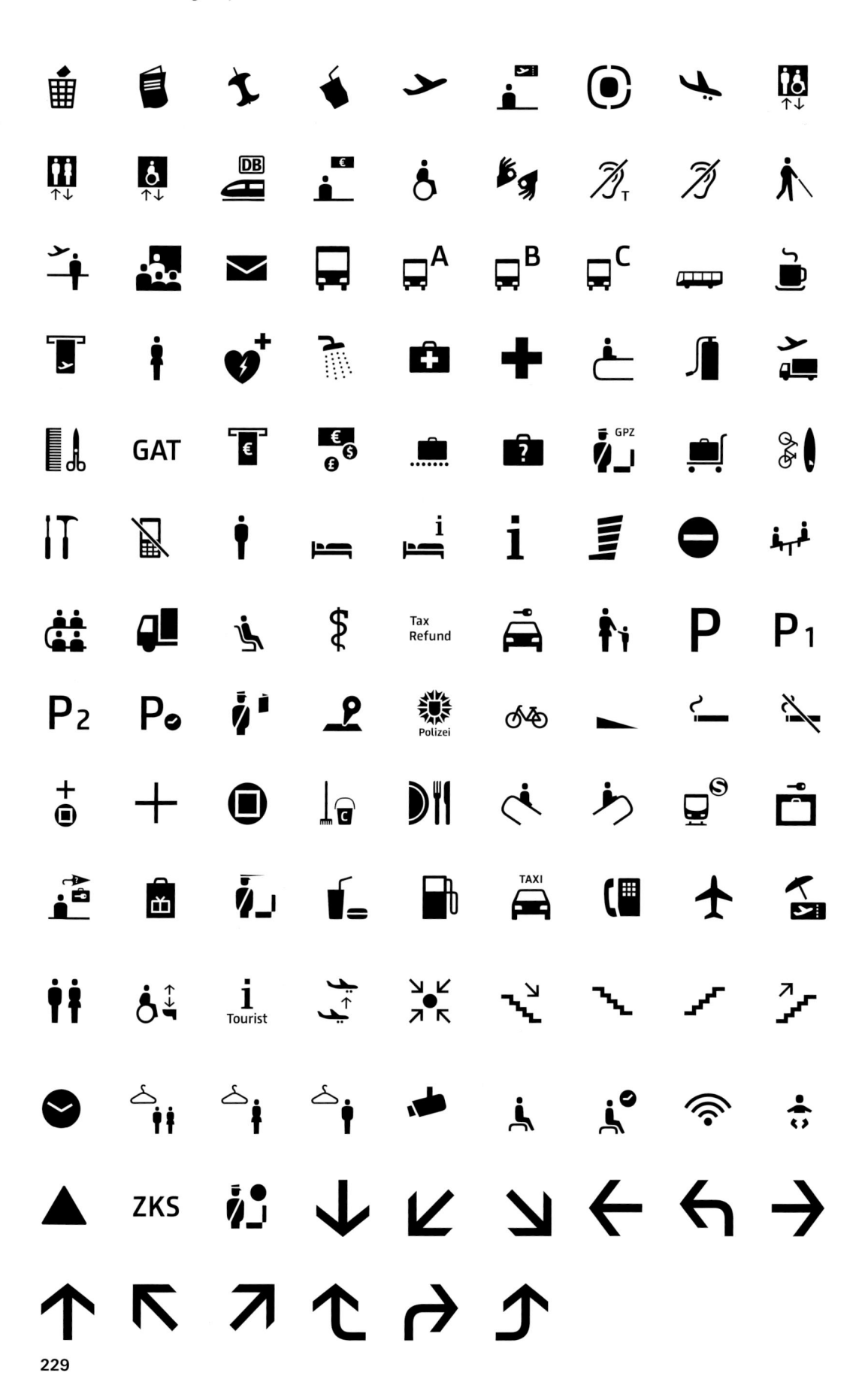

BER Signage Bold
ABCDEFGHIJKL
abcdefghijklm
0123456789

BER Signage Light
ABCDEFGHIJKL
abcdefghijklm
0123456789

Figure 229 Pictograms for Berlin Brandenburg Airport.

Picture 230 BER Font. Design Alexander Branczyk and Georg Seifert on behalf of Schindler Parent.

Airport
Brisbane Airport

There are other ways to make signware for airports. When designing the signage hardware for Brisbane Airport – recently heralded as Australia's most efficient airport – the designers were obviously inspired by aircraft geometry.

The organic, internally lit signs accomodate communication perfectly as well as adding considerably to the identity of the airport.

The graphic design of the signs is divided into two zones, one with written messages and one with large pictograms to be seen from a distance.

The wayshowing system at Brisbane Airport covers the entire passenger experience from parking to gate.

Design 2010
Architecture:
Hassell
Wayshowing:
Frost Design

Figure 231-234 Brisbane Airport.

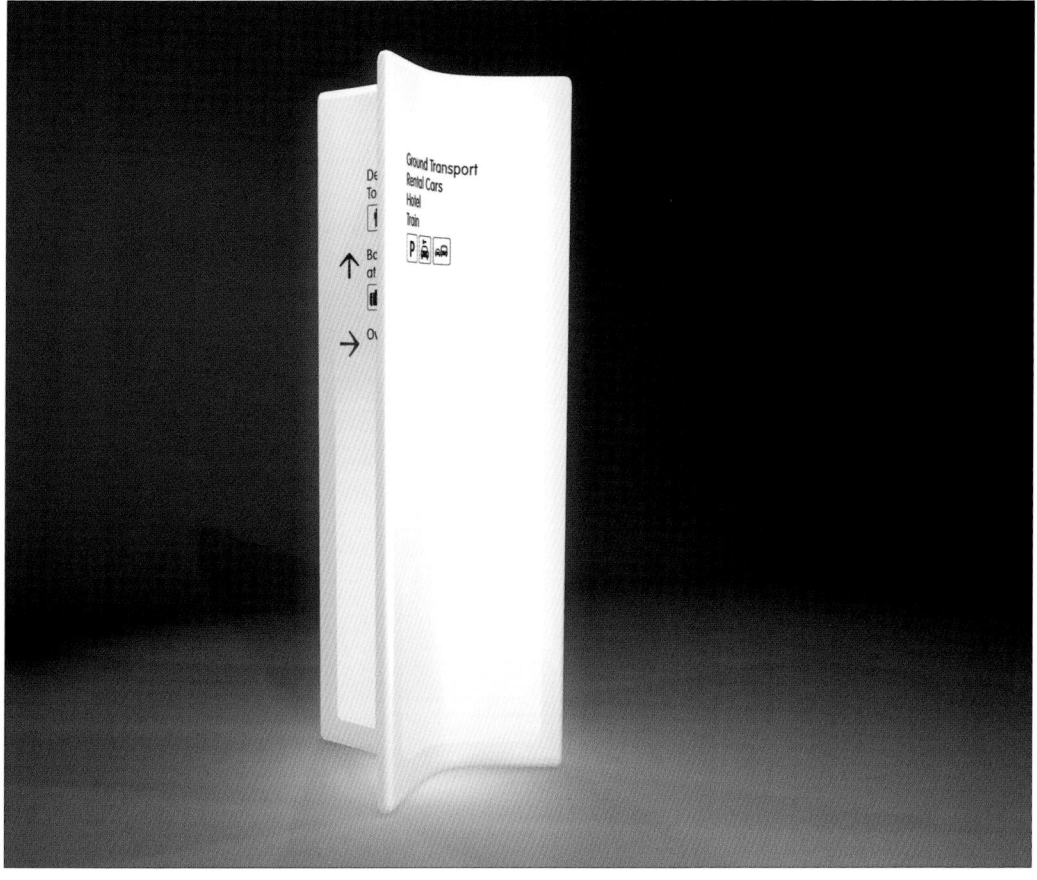

231

232
233
234

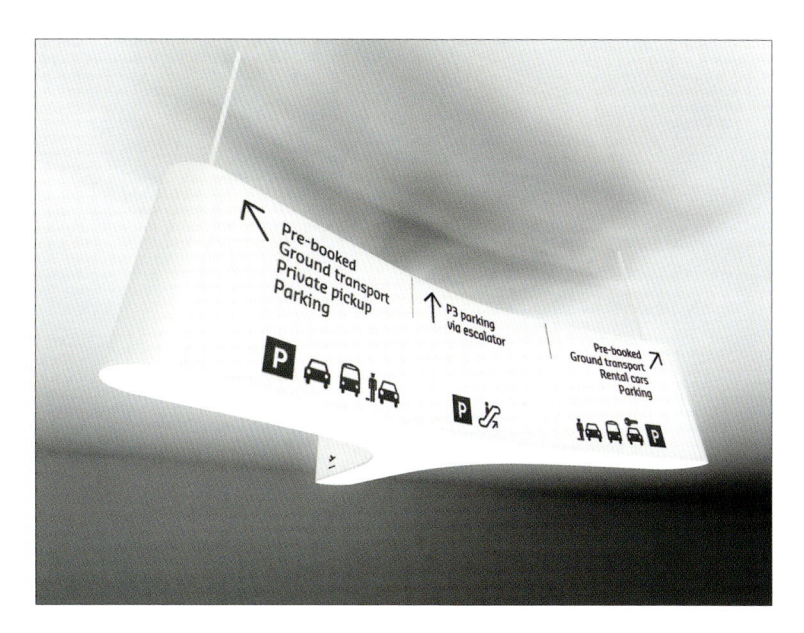

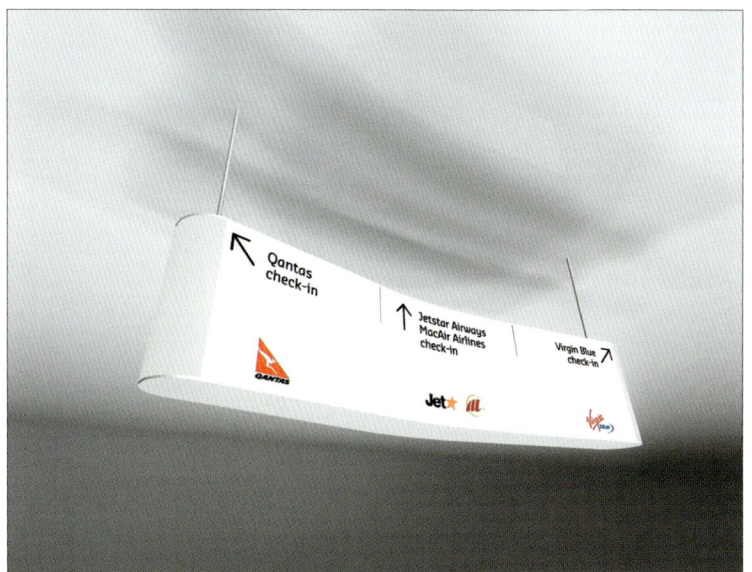

W>W 183

Airport
Qantas check-in

Flying is easy when you are already in the aircraft enjoying your favorite in-flight entertainment. Land operations are the difficult part of the voyage. Serious airports and carriers are aware of this and try to simplify wherever possible.

The Australian airline Qantas has developed a check-in infrastructure that is as much a form of branding as a wayshowing exercise. The design guides travellers on more than one level. Great numbers of passengers with luggage to carry, push, or pull need welcoming messages that they can see swiftly and understand easily.

The new Qantas check-in system has been installed in Melbourne, Perth, and Sydney to date.

Design 2008–
Wayshowing:
Frost Design

Figure 235-241 Qantas 'next generation' check-in.

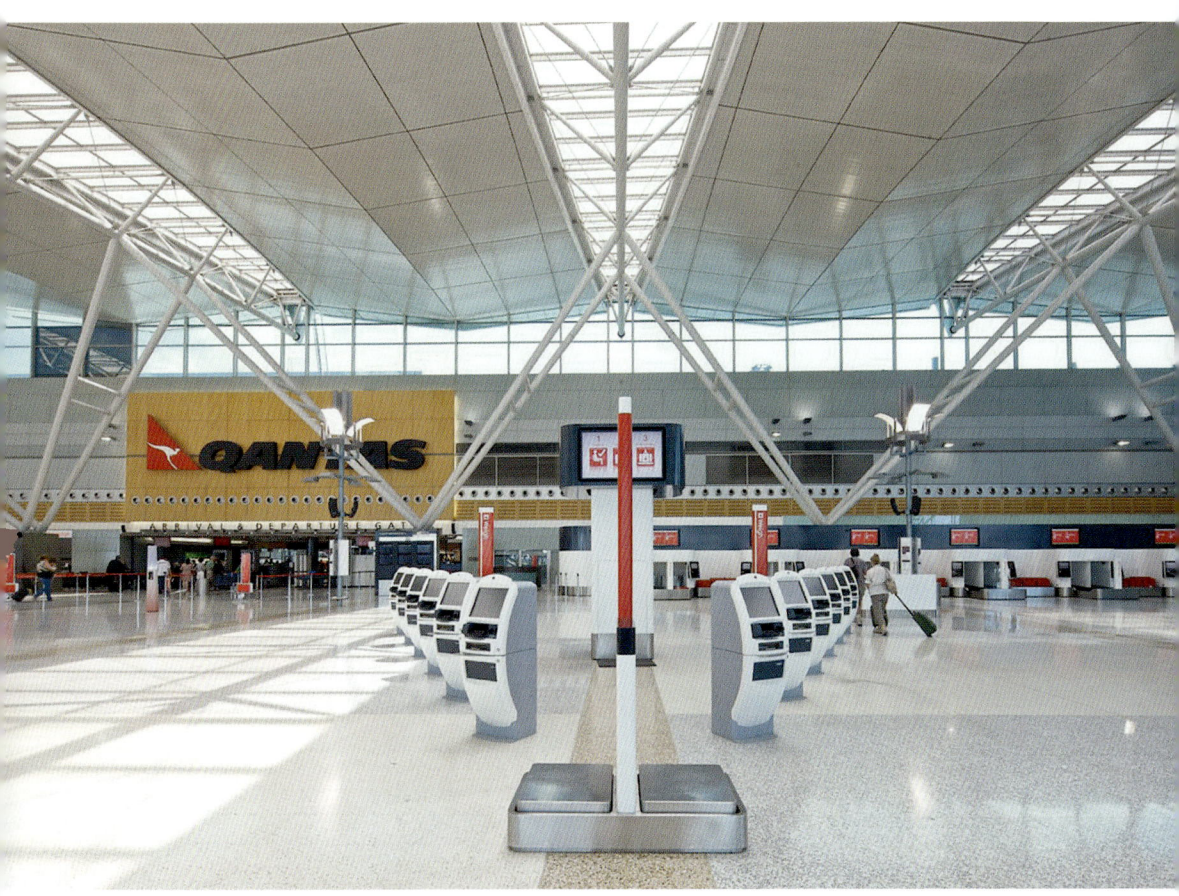

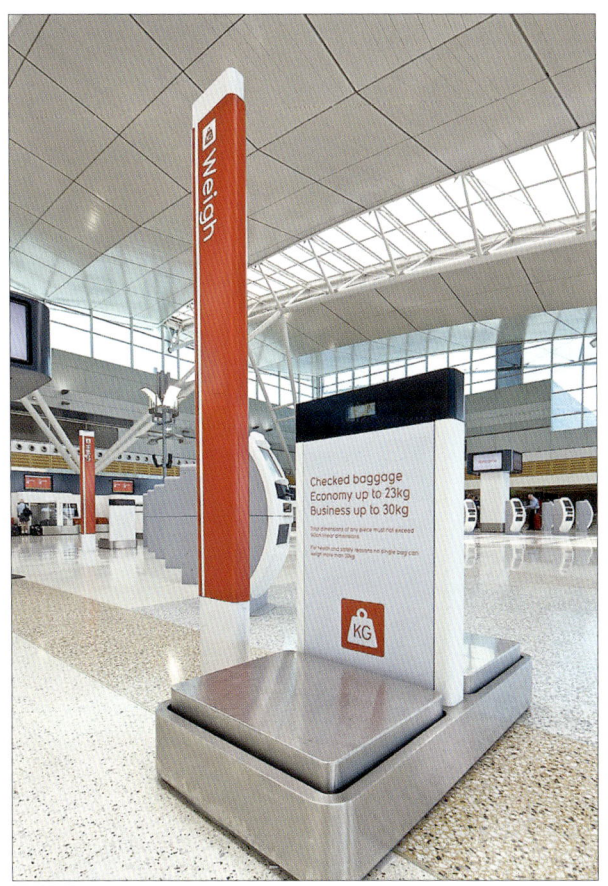

236, 237,
238, 239,
240, 241

Airport
Washington Dulles International Airport

The wayshowing system at Washington Dulles International Airport is consistent with wayshowing systems in the New York airports developed by the same firm. These airport wayshowing systems employ three-colour coding:

Yellow	air transportation
Green	ground transportation
White	other services

The wayshowing goals included:

– facilitating the passenger's path of travel to or from any destination in the airport in the easiest and fastest way possible;
– reducing the sense of stress for all passengers, their companions, and any other users of the airport;
– making users feel as comfortable as possible by providing clear information and instructions;
– doing all of this in a manner that enhances the environment of the airport consistent with airport design heritage and philosophy.

Design 2005-2010
Architecture:
Eero Saarinen (main terminal)
Wayshowing:
Bureau Mijksenaar

Figure 242-244 Washington Dulles International Airport.

242

243
244

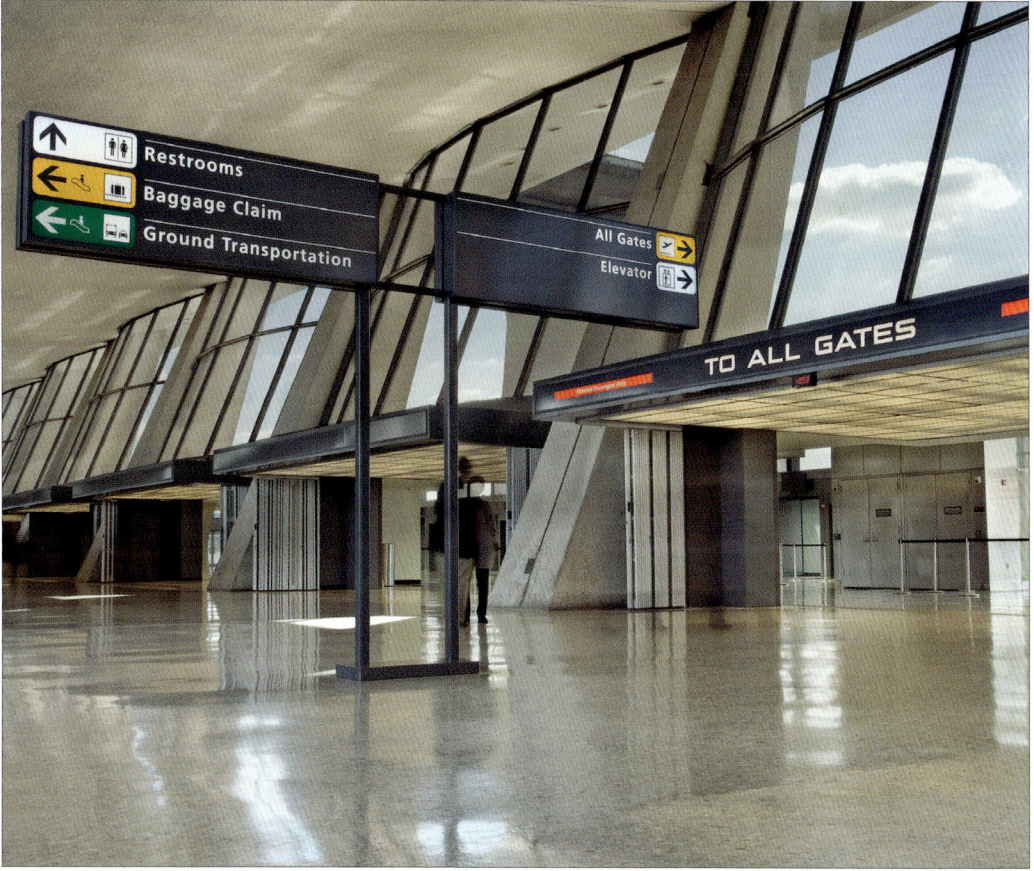

Rail
JR Tokai Shinkansen

When Central Japan Railways / JR Tokai acquired a new full colour LED system for signage with more than ten times higher luminance than previous technology, they put it to good use. They commissioned design for improved readability, focusing on the use of colour and text.

The designer selected the most distinguishable colours among 16.7 million options, designed Latin and Japanese letters for highest legibility on the new displays, and organised their layout for maximum clarity. Everyone benefits from the new design, especially the aged population and people with vision disabilities.

Design 2008
Wayshowing:
Keiichi Koyama

245

Figure 245 The gate board is set above all train doors to display next-train information such as train name, number, time, destination, class, smoking/non-smoking cabins, and stopping stations. Depending on the train operation interval, information on the second-next train, or train not arriving, information is displayed in the lower row. In case of emergency, the board also serves as an emergency information board.

Figure 246 This information system with highly visible colour LEDs also gives audio information. Sequence: Japanese mode > English mode > Train arriving mode.

Figure 247 The font design included signage-specific anti-aliasing to improve letter shape accuracy and legibility.

246

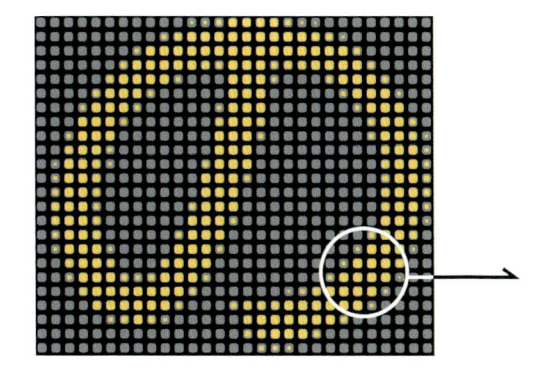

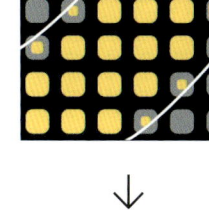

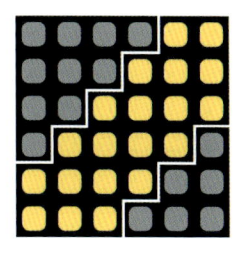

247

W>W 189

Rail
JR Japan Railways, QR codes

JR Japan Railways use QR codes for travel information at the stations. Most Japanese smartphones have a RFID IC tip so that they don't have to read the code but only touch the mark. The JR QR codes carry information such as:

- The name of the station
- A scaleable map of the area around the station
- A list of facilities that can be shown on the map
- Transfer information
- Send message
- Help/FAQ

Design 2008
Wayshowing:
Hyojitou

QR   Quick Response
RFID   Radio Frequency Identification
IC   Integrated Circuit

Figure 248 Japan Railways information wall with QR code (upper right corner).

Figure 249 Scrollable and scalable information read from a QR code and shown on a mobile phone.

Figure 250 Touch by Japanese smartphone with IC tip.

Figure 251 Scan by camera phone.

248

190 W>W

249

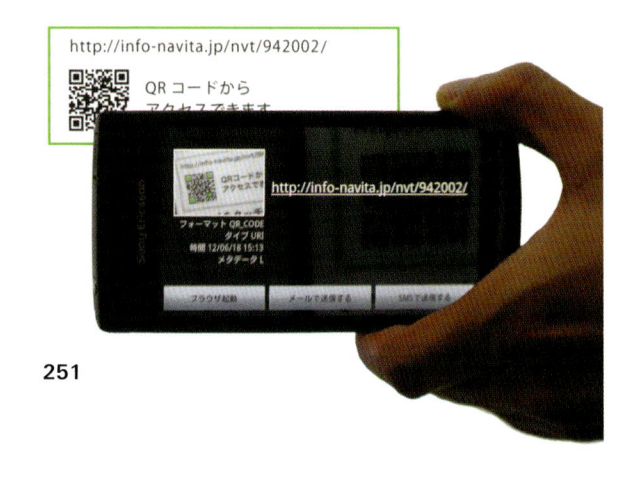

250

251

Rail
MTA, New York

MTA, the New York Metropolitan Transportation Authority, is rolling out a new interactive information system in the subway. It is launching a Beta version at about 90 subway stations, to be extended later to all of the 400+ stations. The front end of the system includes 47 inch touch screens with line maps and other pictorial and textual information.

When planning the content, Control Group had three user groups in mind: routine daily commuters, off-routine commuters, and tourists. Based on these user groups, Control Group identified ten scenarios, where travellers need information. A typical scenario is 'off-routine commuter who has planned a new excursion or trip and is looking to get somewhere new'.

The top of the screen identifies the station and the lines serving it. The next part gives real-time timetable information including scheduled trains and information about irregularities. One touch on another station on the screen map brings up the route to that station on the map and an accompanying text field with all relevant information about necessary changes.

The system is far from fully developed, but several services are envisioned. Among them, tourists will enjoy seasonally adjusted placeshowing.

The system can also retrieve information from the station. In principle, camera and microphones at stations will enable two-way communication and capture information about commuter density and more.

Design 2013
Wayshowing:
Control Group

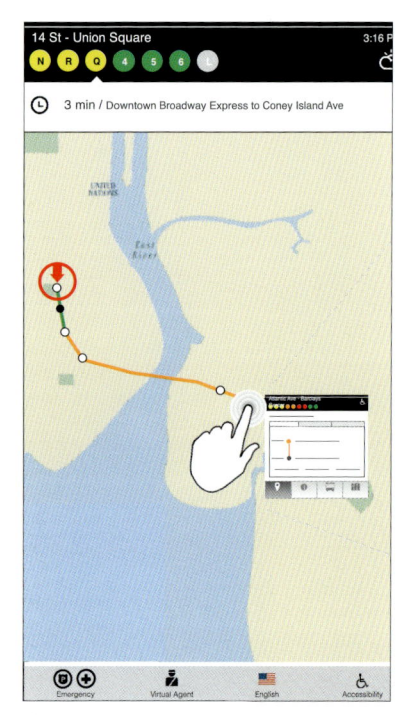

253

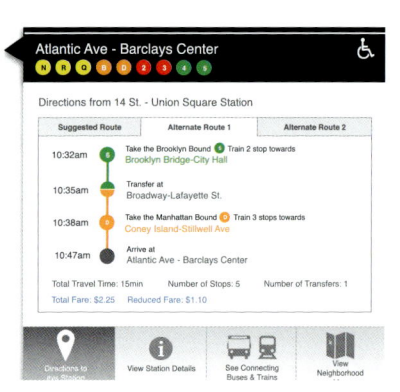

254

252

Figure 252-255 Touch screens. New York subway. MTA.

Atlantic Ave – Barclays Center

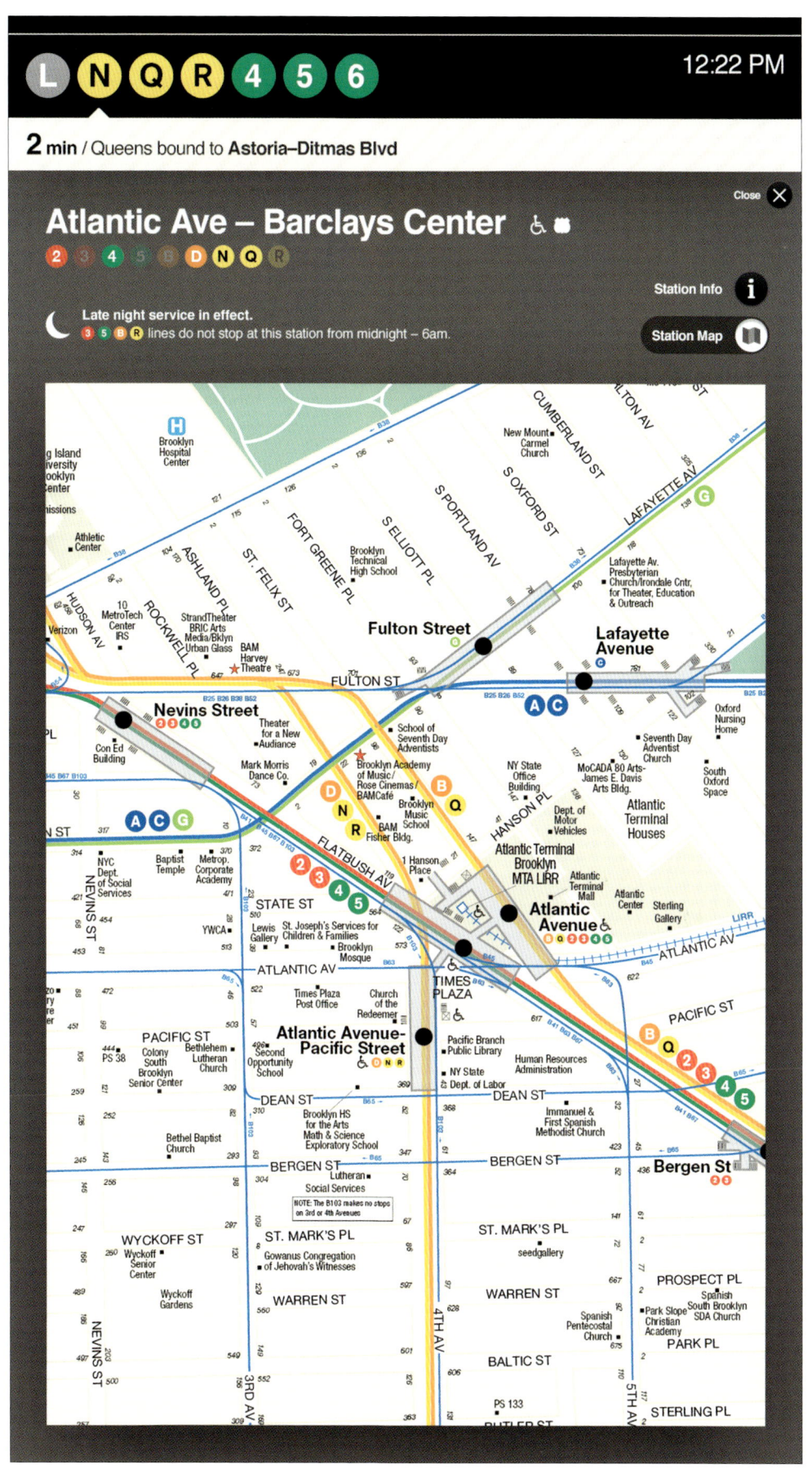

L N Q R 4 5 6 — 12:22 PM

2 min / Queens bound to Astoria–Ditmas Blvd

2 3 4 5 D N Q R

Late night service in effect.
3 5 B R lines do not stop at this station from midnight – 6am.

Station Info

Station Map

Rail
NSB Norwegian State Railways

Terminal operations are often the most troublesome wayfinding discipline. In Norwegian train stations, a new environment, lots of luggage (Norwegians often bring their skis), and short transfer times between connections all add up. When travelling by train, finding the station and the right platform is not enough. Because trains are long, sometimes running more than 200 metres, knowing which car you are in and finding it are essential.

NSB Norwegian State Railways have tackled this problem by using platform monitors that indicate the various cars in a train and state their location on marked sections of the platform. The platform has marks every five metres.

Egalitarian Norway does not have first class train cars. Instead, stars mark cars with extra comfort.

Design 2013
Project management:
Bent Flyen
Design:
Lise Haakestad

Figure 256-257 A long time has passed since train passengers were addressed with handwriting or Modulex boards.

Figure 258 The main board at Oslo Central Station.

Figure 259 Norwegians often bring their skis when travelling by train. This creates platform congestion.

Figure 260-261 Platform monitor. The grey part of the train is not accessible. Pictograms explain what is where.

256
257

258
259

261

260

W>W 195

City
TriMet Portland Transit Mall

This wayshowing project in the Portland, Oregon downtown office, retail, and cultural centre does more than show the way. It is a vital part of a general re-vamp of the downtown business area that includes introducing a light rail service along an existing bus mall. Alternating bus and light rail platforms follow the same curb line.

To create life and revitalise retail business along the transit mall streets, Portland replaced old transit shelters and furnishings that created dark areas and obstructed streets.

Wayshowing elements are carefully layered on steel-clad pylons in order to enable long distance identification, as well as transport information to be read at a short distance. The latter part includes real-time LCD monitors. CCTV cameras also play a part in the urban environment.

The environmental graphic design perspective was allowed to influence architectural, urban design, and civil engineering work.

Design 2009
Wayfinding:
Mayer / Reed

Figure 262 Pylon at light train platform.

Figure 263 Bus pylon.

Figure 264 Rail pylon.

Figure 265 Real-time LCD monitor.

Figure 266 Tactile transit stop sign.

262

263

264

265

266

City
Trade Fair Stuttgart

The wayshowing design of Trade Fair Stuttgart is a colourful affair. The colours take wayfinding visitors by the hand, while providing the venue with a distinctive visual identity. Red signs lead to exhibition halls, pink signs to the conference centre, and blue signs to the exit.

The colours of the striped signboards are designed with limited internal contrast to let letters, numbers, and arrows take the foreground. The upright Futura-like Avenir typeface designed by Adrian Frutiger in 1988 stays perfectly clear of the stripes. Baselines, x-lines, and cap-lines never coincide with the stripe edges.

Where signboards would clash with the architecture, colours, letters, numbers, and arrows are painted directly on the walls. Translucent film is used on glass.

Design 2008
Architecture:
Wulf & Partner
Wayshowing:
büro uebele

Figure 267-269 Trade Fair Stuttgart.

267

W>W 199

City
Eureka Parking, Melbourne

There are wayshowing commissions where the only concern is to show the way from A to B as clearly as possible. There are also wayshowing commissions where creating an identity and a memorable experience wildly overshadows the naked wayshowing problem. Gary Emery's design office, Emery Studio, solves the latter kind of commission with conspicuous solutions.

Emery Studio's wayshowing system for Eureka Parking, the car park under Melbourne's tallest building fits the above description. It is as much about experience and identity as it is about wayshowing. Nobody leaves the space without remembering that they were there.

Design 2006
Architecture:
Fender Katsalidis Architects
Wayshowing:
Emery Studio

Figure 270-273 Eureka Parking. Melbourne.

271
272
273

City
Water Formula, Laboratório Central, Lisbon

The wayshowing arrangement in this modernist laboratory building is much more than wayshowing. It provides a memorable experience that is appropriate for a visit to this very special place.

The overall use of a clear water-associated blue colour serves a double function. Applied on only one side of corridors and intersections it guides. For instance, in the parking space, the blue walls are always on the driver's side.

A marriage of crisp typography and chemical formulas showing directions and locations confirms the purpose of the building. This extends to the building's abbreviated name: Lab C. The wayshowing process led to the linguistic identity of the building.

Design 2010
Architecture:
Gonçalo Byrne Arquitectos
Wayshowing:
P-06 Atelier with Global landscape architects

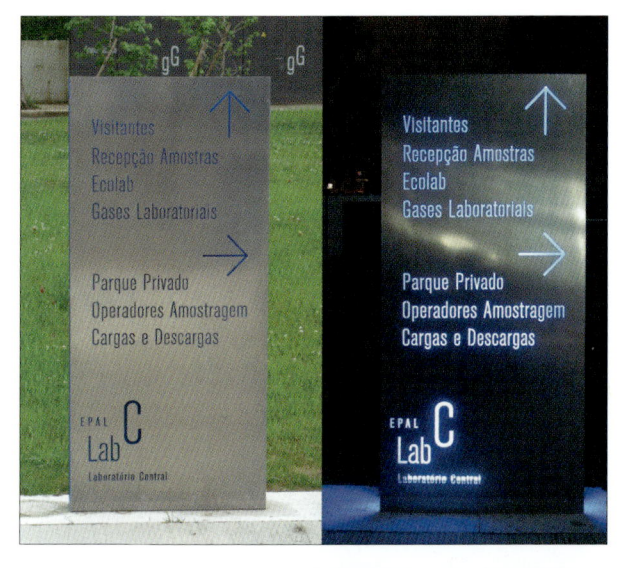

Figure 274-278 Water Formula. Lisbon.

Figure 274-275 Exterior signage.

Figure 276-277 Corridors.

Figure 278 Parking.

276
277

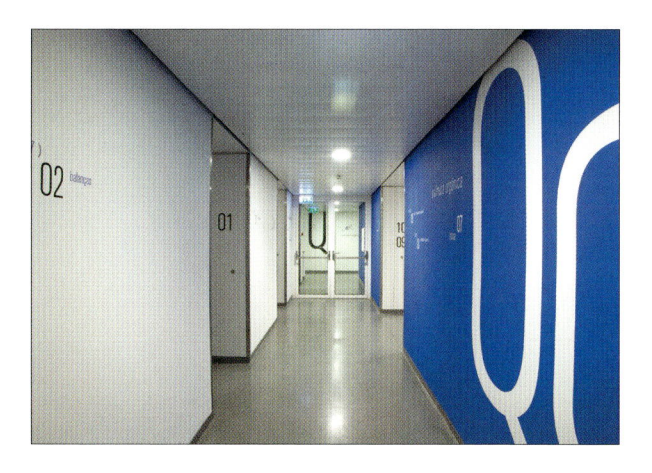

278

W>W 203

City
Escaping a tsunami, Santa Barbara

Wayfinding is sometimes a matter of life and death. In these situations, wayfinding demands preparedness as well as wayshowing. Wayfinding favours the prepared wayfarer. That is the case in the event of a tsunami. When the tsunami is already ashore, it may be too late to learn what to do and where to go. People involved don't have much time and are possibly not in a state where they are able to learn effectively.

In Santa Barbara, California, authorities have taken action to prepare citizens and help everybody present in the event of a tsunami. Based on knowledge about which areas may be flooded, authorities have planned escape routes and prepared information material for those concerned.

Developing the new information model involved thinking of four possible information reading situations: Leisure, Direct, Urgent, and Emergency.

The idea behind the new model is to inform the public, visitors, and residents prior to an evacuation instead of waiting until the urgent stage. Early information meets its audience when they are better capable to understand and learn, allowing them to take precautions, develop cognitive maps, and combine them with possible previous experiences before an evacuation.

The information media include brochures distributed to households, flyers for boats, and signs with escape maps in the streets.

Design 2012
Study:
Claudine Jaenichen, Tavish Ryan, Marissa Bredice, and Steve Schandler.
Design:
Claudine Jaenichen

Reading situations

– Leisure
Individuals are able to process information voluntarily with minimal anxiety.

– Direct
Individuals process an instruction or notice a change in environment but are not necessarily threatened or limited by time.

– Urgent
Individuals process information with alertness within various levels of anxiety and time limitations.

– Emergency
Individuals are immediately affected by the environment in a threatening way, resulting in less time to process information, reading, and comprehension susceptible to tunnel vision*, and temporary cognitive paralysis.

* The term 'tunnel vision' is here used to describe a temporary cognitive response, not as used in the chapter on visual impairments to describe peripheral field loss.

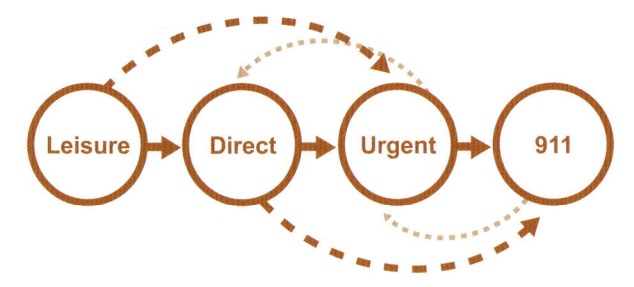

279

280

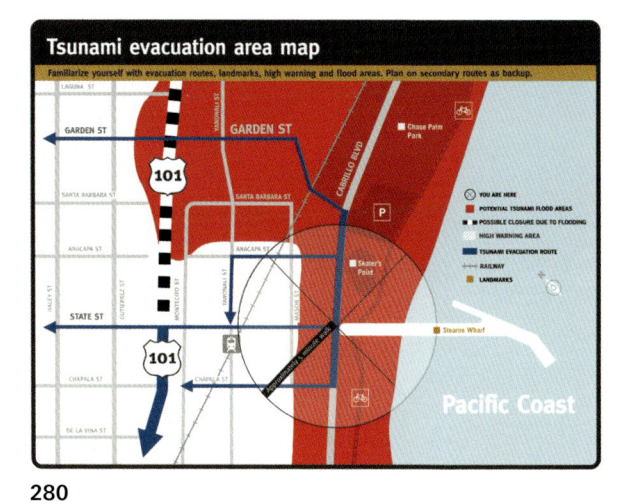

281

282

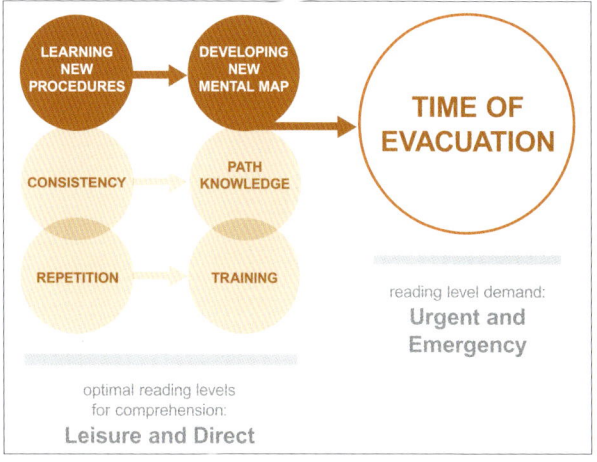

283

Figure 279 Reading situations.

Figure 280-281 Evacuation map.

Figure 282 Previous information model. Distribution of information given at time of evacuation.

Figure 283 New information model with information campaign prior to evacuation.

W>W 205

Knowledge
Vancouver Community Library

Locating the children's book section in the public library doesn't have the same urgency as finding the emergency ward in the hospital. Still, we want to find it easily, without much thinking, and without involving the staff.

The Vancouver Community Library provides wayshowing that both facilitates easy wayfinding and signals the open-minded attitude of the place. The LIBRARY spelling letters in front of the building and signature markings under the landings connote user-friendliness.

Design 2010
Architecture:
The Miller Hull Partnership, LLP
Wayshowing:
Mayer / Reed

285

284

Figure 284 Vancouver Community Library. USA.

Figure 285 Painted super graphics on the atrium stairwell provide a quick understanding of the library organisation.

Figure 286 View from the base of the main stairwell showing the wayshowing hierarchy.

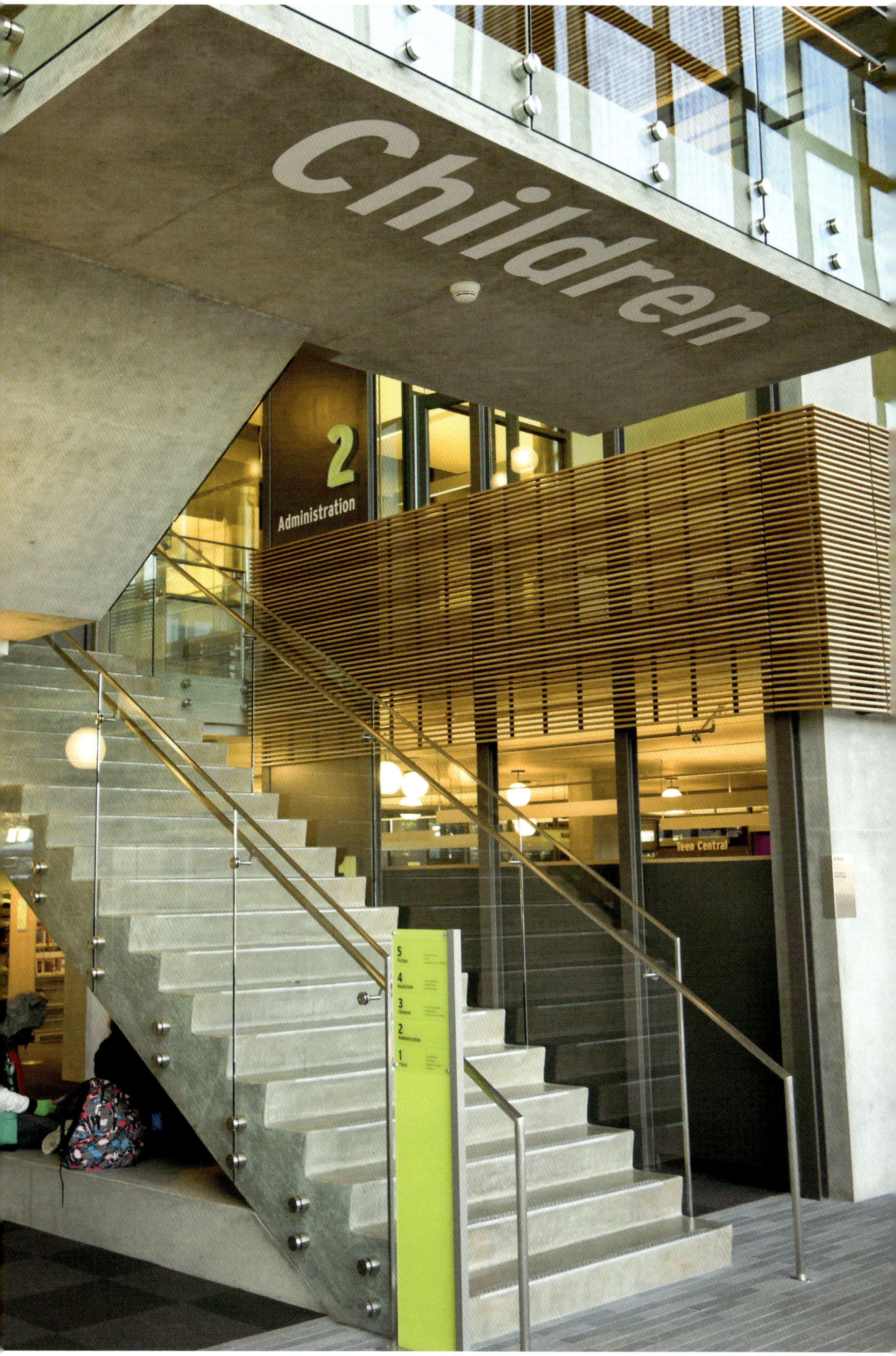
Children
2
Administration
Teen Central

Knowledge
The State Library of New South Wales, Sydney

The interrobang logo of the State Library of New South Wales indicates a love of print and books. The interrobang is a seldom-seen punctuation mark that marries a question mark and an exclamation mark. It unites question and answer, a most appropriate sign for a library.

The delicate wayshowing signage with empire type on a white background is an important part of a comprehensive branding operation based on extensive research.

Design 2010
Architecture:
GAO
Wayshowing:
Frost Design

Figure 287-290 The State Library of New South Wales.

287

288
289
290

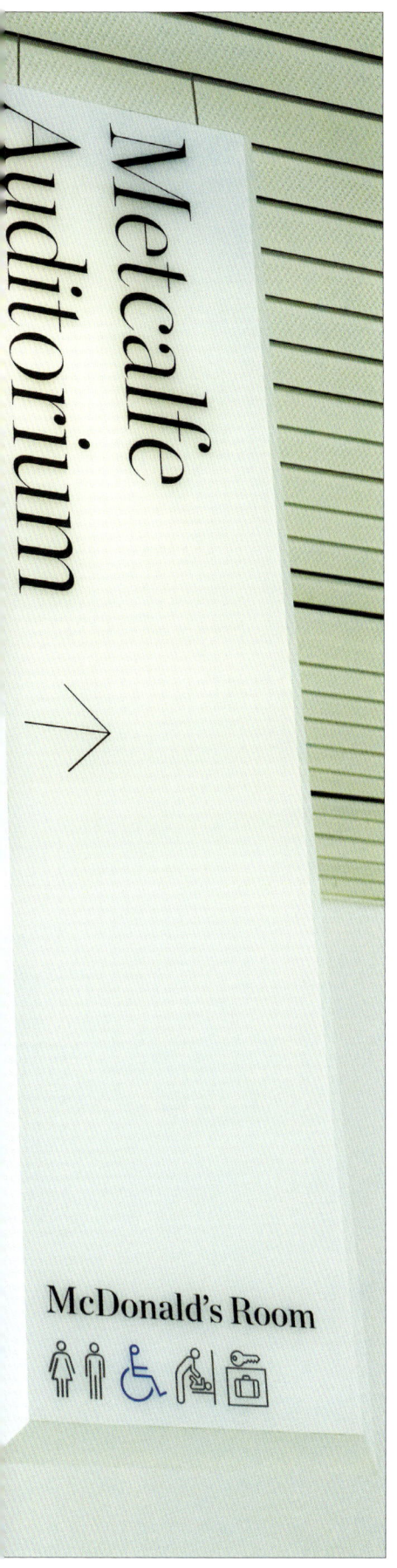

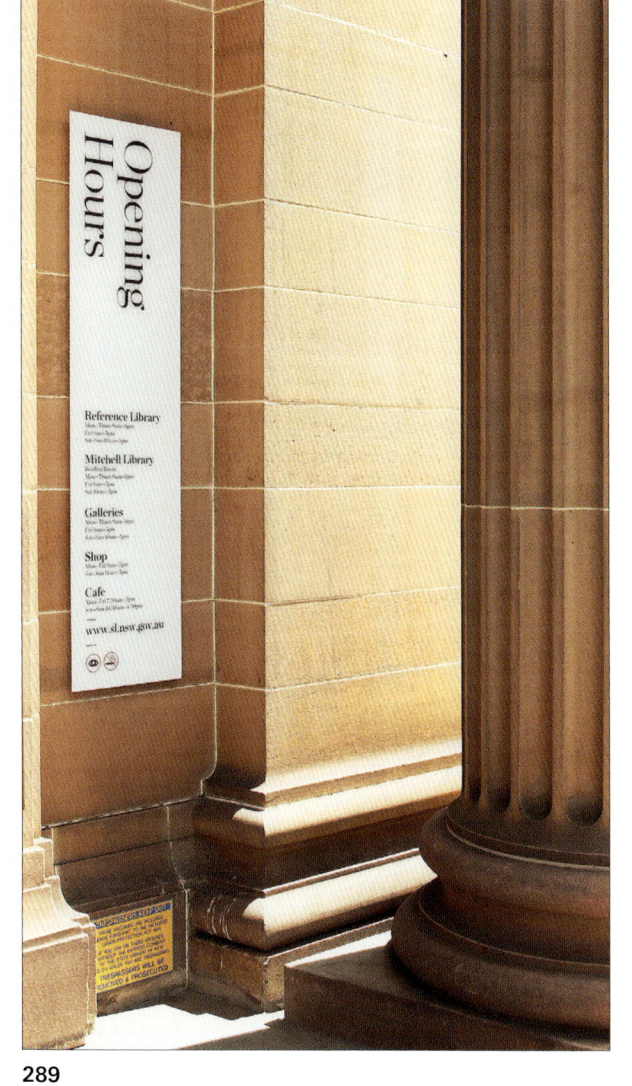

Knowledge
Upper Austrian Federal State Library, Linz

When this library – originally built in the 1930s – was rebuilt and expanded it also got a new wayfinding system. The designers wanted to pay respect to times gone by using the Blender Western Latin typeface. The angular information carriers that protrude from the wall are both discreet and conspicuous. The playful type and whiteness of the wayshowing design is congenial with the library atmosphere. It says: Have fun, but don't shout.

Design 2009
Architecture:
Bez + Kock
Wayshowing:
bauer – konzept & gestaltung

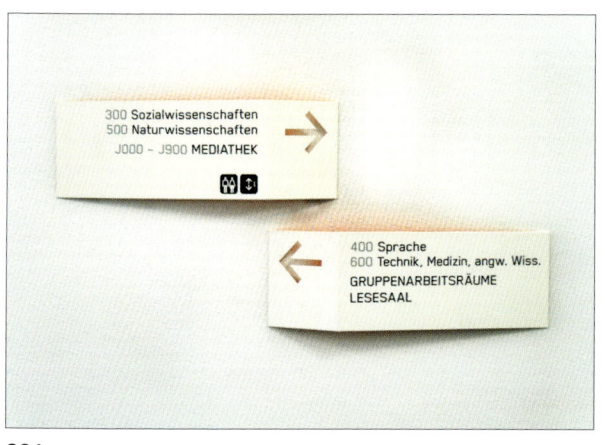

Figure 291-294 Upper Austrian Federal State Library. Linz.

291
292
293

900 Geschichte und Geografie

800 Literatur und Literaturwissenschaften

600 Technik, Medizin, Angew. Wissenschaften

400 Sprache
500 Naturwissenschaften

100 Philosophie und Psychologie
200 Theologie

000 Informatik, Informationswissenschaften, Allgemeine Werke

Knowledge
British Library, London

The British Library, the national library of the United Kingdom, houses 150 million items, including 44 million books. Book-loving visitors get a booklet that – together with free-standing and wall-mounted directories and existing signage – shows their way up and down. The maps in the booklet play a major role in the wayshowing process. If there is a literate – and map-literate – audience anywhere, it is here.

Design 2009-2010
Architecture (1997):
Colin St John Wilson
Wayshowing:
(vertical & maps)
Holmes Wood

Figure 295-296 British Library, London.

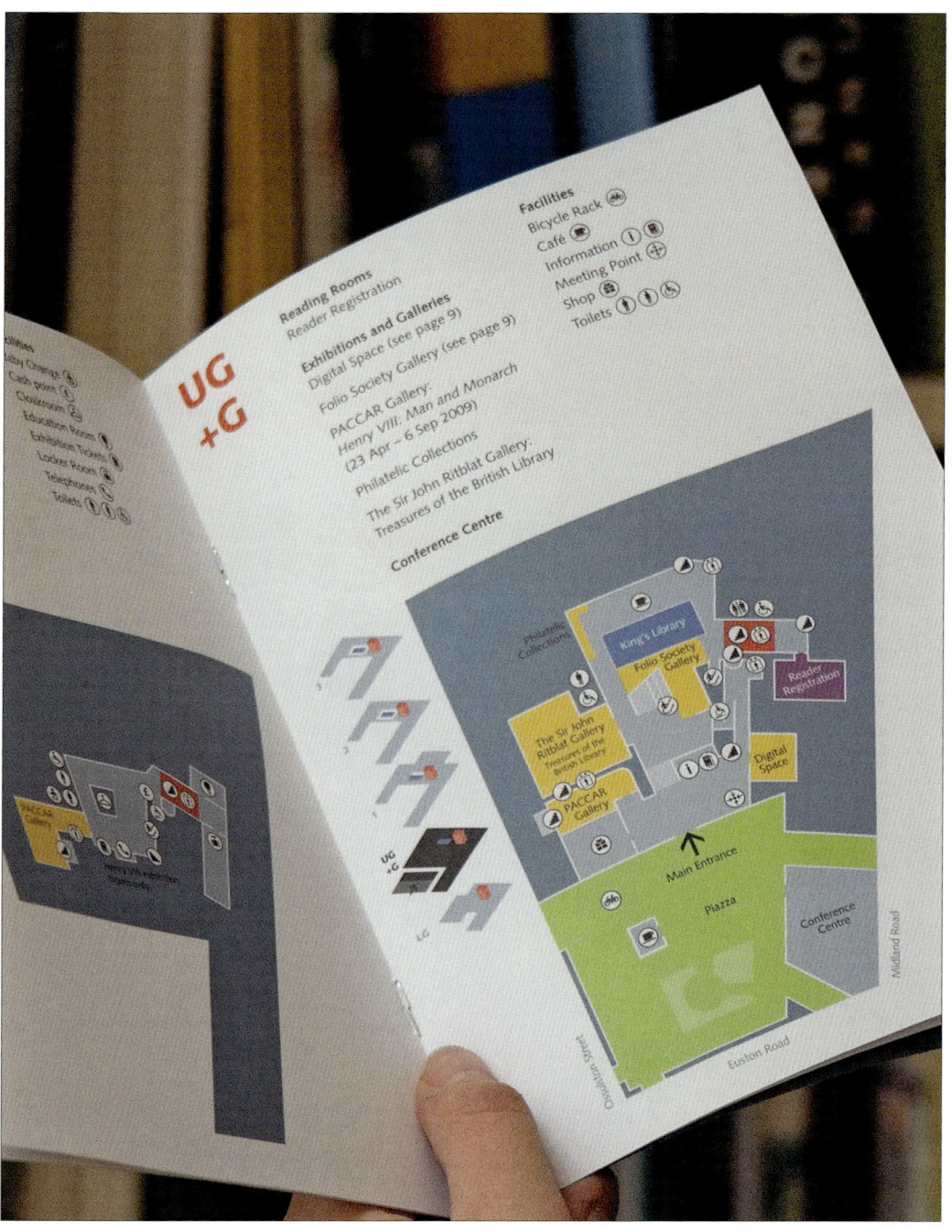

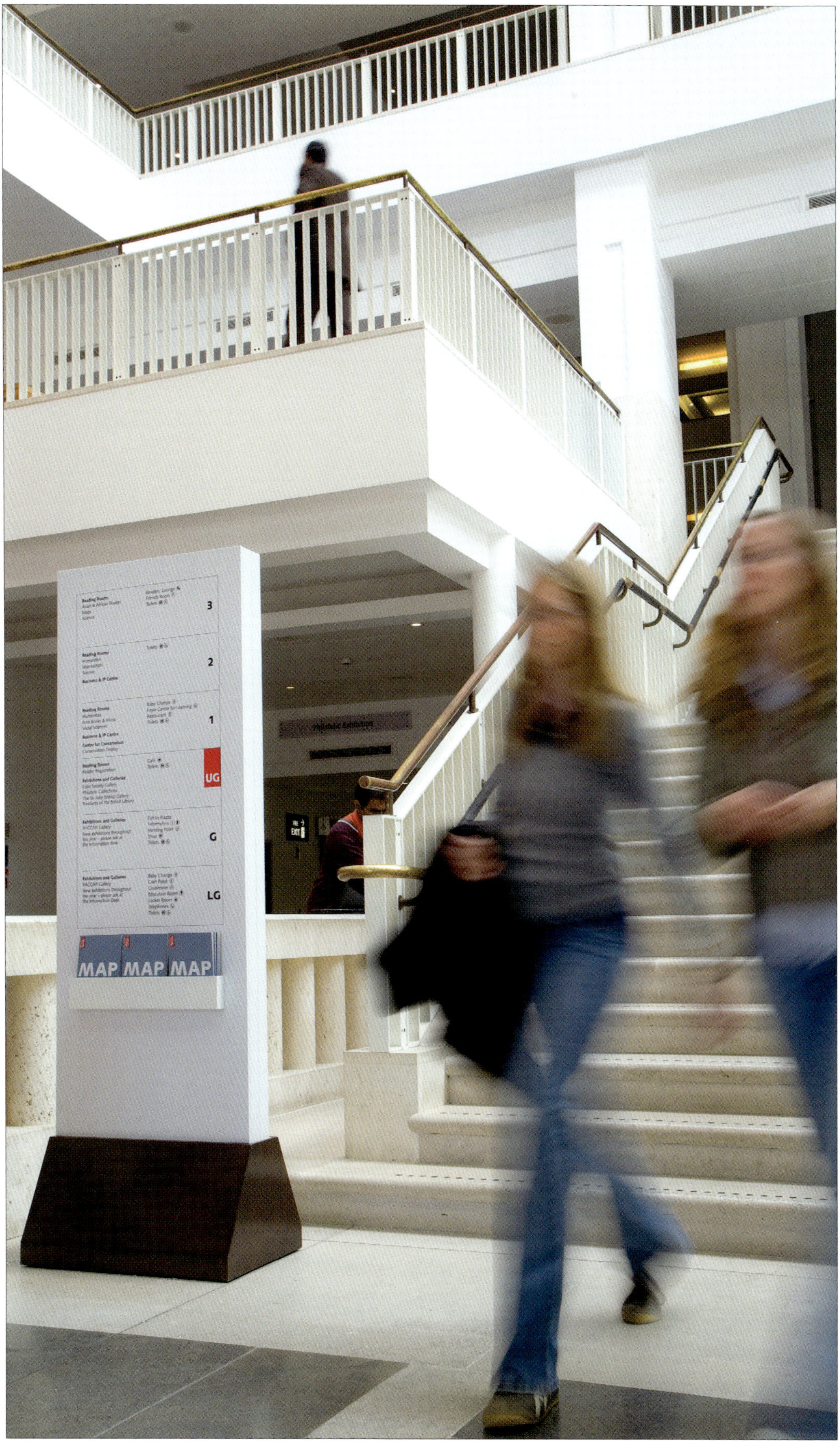
3
2
1
UG
G
LG
MAP
MAP
MAP

Knowledge
Osnabrück University of Applied Science

At Osnabrück University of Applied Science in Germany, the signs are not vandalised or obstructed as they are at some universities. The wayshowing signs, including words, numbers, and pictograms, are painted on the ceilings. Stargazers and others look up to find their way in the didactic establishment. Signage for upwardly mobile youth?

Design 2004
Architecture:
Jockers Architekten
Wayshowing:
büro uebele

Figure 297-299 Osnabrück University of Applied Science. Germany.

297
298

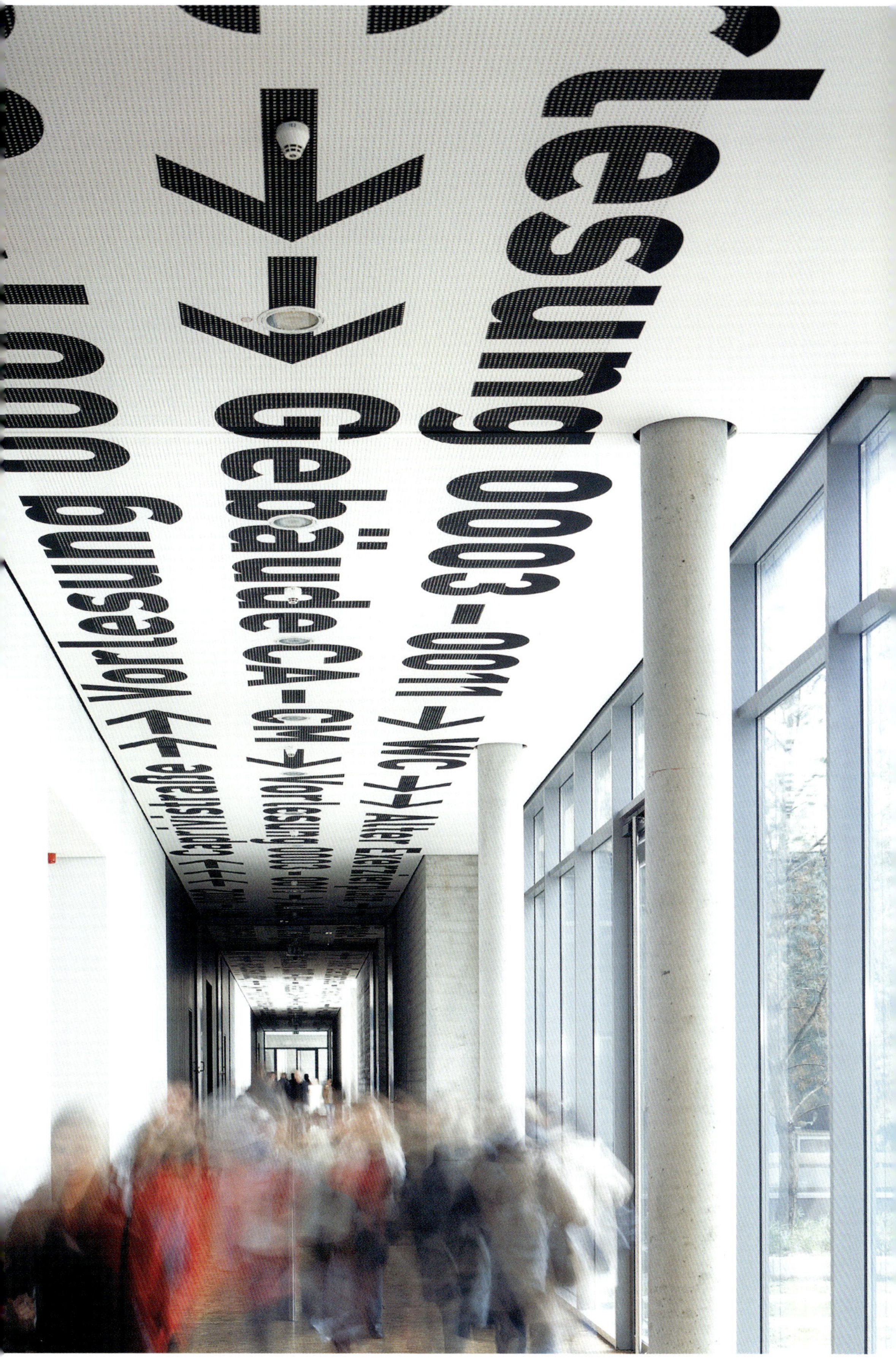
Vorlesung 0003 - 0011
Gebäude CA - CM

Culture
Auckland Art Gallery, Toi o Tamaki

The designers of the wayshowing system of the Auckland Art Gallery in New Zealand, designed both the museum's visual brand identity and its graphic wayshowing, but they maintained a sharp divide between branding and signage throughout the building.

The visual branding including outdoor banners is a high-profiled play on the word and the letters ART. The colours are limited to the three primary signal colours, red, black, and white.

Outdoors and indoors, building signage is pared down to go with the 1887 faux French Renaissance building and a 2011 delicate, highly transparent expansion that doubled the exhibition space. Wayshowing messages are clear, but signage is the servant, not the master.

A recessive and flexible approach was taken that would work through both building types and be sensitive to surface materials including white walls, basalt stone, native Kauri timber, and acres of glass. Elements of the system were designed to be easily updated with a changing gallery programme.

Two types of directional signage are deployed depending on surface material.

Typography on white or coloured walls is set-out in screen printed grey vinyl, or contrasting white vinyl. On basalt stone walls, 3mm stainless steel is applied.

All typography is set in Theinhardt, a grotesk typeface designed by Swiss typographer François Rappo. A suite of symbols were designed to integrate with the type.

Design 2011
Architecture:
FJMT + Archimedia
Wayshowing:
ALT Group

300

Figure 300-303 Auckland Art Gallery.

Café
Māori portraits
New Zealand historic art
International contemporary art
Exhibitions
International historic art

Entry
Shop
New Zealand collection
North atrium
Administration

303

Espresso bar
New Zealand contemporary art
Sculpture terraces
Members lounge

Victorian art

Research Library

301
302

W>W 217

Culture
Maritime Museum Rotterdam

When showing the way, graphic designers working with signage in museums have several options. One option is to concentrate on making placeshowing and wayshowing as effective as possible by telling visitors what can be found and how to find it with minimum fuss. In this option, they make the signage visible for those who need it, but not conspicuous enough to kill everything else.

In addition to strictly functional concerns, graphic designers can design a signage system that matches the architecture and becomes a natural extension of the building.

Last, graphic designers can adjust their signage to the theme of the museum, making it congenial with contents and message.

The graphic wayshowing of the Maritime Museum in Rotterdam works along all three avenues: strict functionality; greyish signs with angular shapes that harmonise with the building; and vermillion accents that carry a scent.

Design 2010
Architecture:
Wim Quist, 1900s
Renovation:
Ramin Visch
Wayshowing:
Bureau Mijksenaar

Figure 304-306 Maritime Museum Rotterdam.

304
305

Deck 0

Tentoonstellingen ↗
Exhibitions

Museumbibliotheek
Museum library

Museumschip 'Buffel' →
Museum ship 'Buffel'

Museumcafé
Museum cafe

M1319

Culture
TAP — Théâtre et Auditorium Poitiers

The concept for the wayshowing system at Théâtre et Auditorium Poitiers took its inspiration from the Dada movement. Words and letters are freely arranged and partially expressed in a 'dadaistic' way. The building is literally a container for words and sounds.

The guidance system consists of oversized letters and numerals recognisable from a distance. Exterior video projections onto the glass 'skin' of the building announce current and upcoming events.

Design 2006-2008
Architecture:
JLCG Arquitectos
Wayshowing:
P-06 Atelier

Figure 307-310 Théâtre et Auditorium, Poitiers, France.

Figure 307 Parking.

Figure 308 Artists' foyer.

Figure 309-310 Foyer.

307
308

220 W>W

309
310

Culture
Royal Botanic Gardens, Kew

The Royal Botanic Gardens at Kew in the United Kingdom, best known as Kew Gardens, are the ideal subject for a smartphone app. Kew Gardens are moving, and they are large. The Gardens change with the seasons, and every day there is something new to see somewhere on the 121 hectares. 'See today' tells what to look for and where. The area makes it sensible to know precisely how to find chosen targets, and the map enables it.

On a tour of the Gardens, the smartphone comes in handy for reading 'dig deeper' information given by QR codes and Augmented Reality. The app has a QR scanner as well as an AR reader.

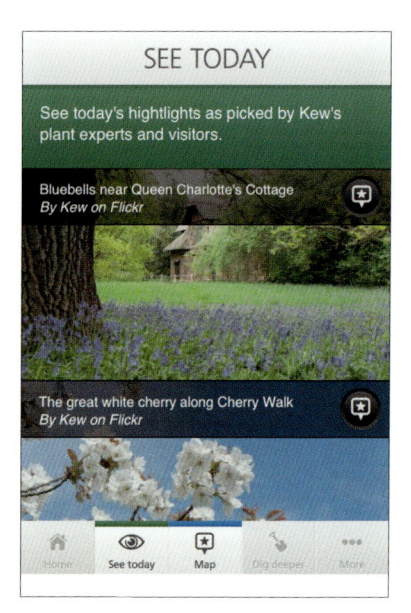

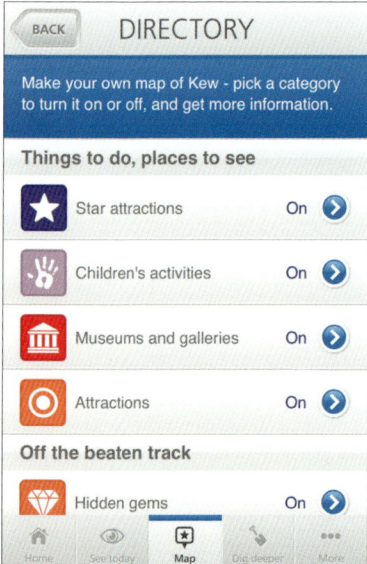

Design 2013
Design:
Make it Clear
Make it Digital

Figure 311-319 Kew Gardens app.

Figure 314 Kew Gardens app. Map customised to show See today and Hidden gems.

Figure 315 Augmented Reality identifying Turkey oak in glasshouse.

Figure 316 Ananas plant with QR code.

Figure 317 The QR code of the Ananas plant read by an iPhone.

311, 312
313

222 W>W

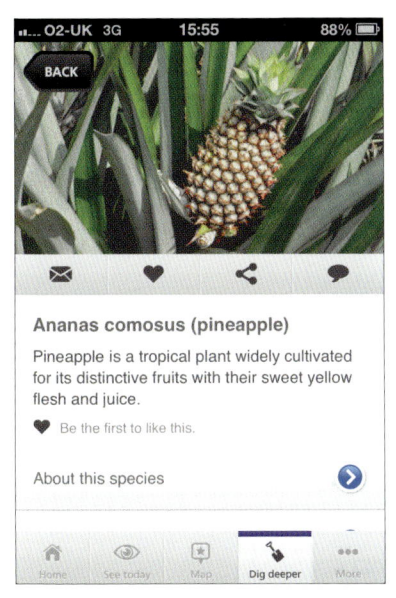

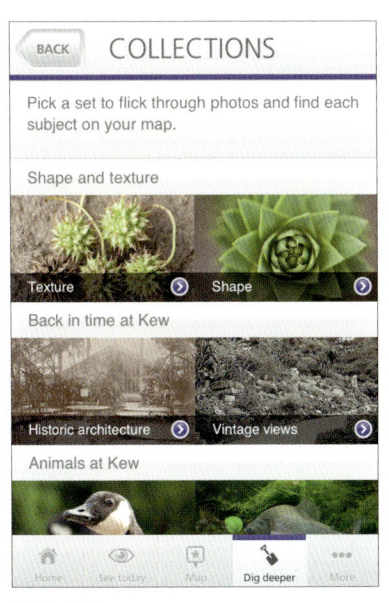

314, 315
316, 317
318, 319

Outdoor
Bikeway, Lisbon

The 7,362-metre bikeway along the river Tagus in Lisbon offers more than half an hour's ride from one end to the other. The graphic marking of the route adds to the experience of the different urban spaces passed. Cyclists are both directed and surprised while pedaling on, along, and against changing messages such as poems by Alberto Caeiro and onomatopoeia – sound describing words – while passing under bridges.

Design 2010
Wayshowing:
P-06 Atelier with Global landscape architects

Figure 320-323 Bikeway, Lisbon.

Figure 320 Vertical interventions.

Figure 321 Onomatopoeic intervention under the bridge.

Figure 322 Pavement marks (detail).

Figure 323 Beginning / End of the track.

320
321

322
323

W>W 225

Outdoor
Melbourne Park

How do you signpost an area around several sports arenas where everything is largest and loudest? One way is to play the-china-in-the-elephant-shop and address the sports spectators with graphics that stand out because of their un-brutal appearance. Gary Emery did just that in Melbourne Park, a centrally located sports compound that houses the Australia Open tennis tournament.

The wayshowing system comprises fingerposts, flat-mounted, and protruding signs.

Design 2010
Wayshowing:
Emery Studio

324

325

Figure 324-330 Melbourne Park.

226 W>W

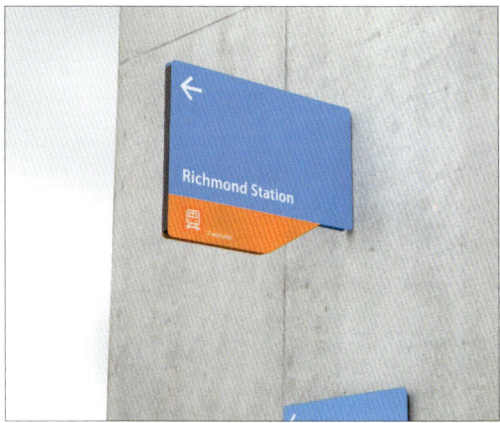

326, 327
328, 329

330

W>W 227

Outdoor
Falls Creek Alpine Resort

Falls Creek is a snow sport resort in the Victorian highlands 350 kilometres northeast of Melbourne. When finding their way, visitors are occasionally met by reduced visibility due to snow, fog, and darkness, conditions that call for highly conspicuous wayshowing.

The local system of fingerposts and related signs responds unequivocally to this context. The safety connoting orange sign elements provide authority as well as visibility. They say: 'Watch these signs carefully.'

Falls Creek is also used for mountain biking and hiking during the summer months. The two seasons demand a flexible sign system, since not all signs apply to both seasons. The modular sign system built around standard 70mm steel poles enables easy seasonal module change by the resort staff.

The organic visual language of the sign branches and stems allegedly emulates the shape of local eucalyptus trees. The typeface Sauna was chosen for its legibility and organic feel.

Design 2008
Wayshowing:
Büro North

331

Figure 331-333 Falls Creek wayshowing. The branch like forms and shifting vertical forms were developed to allow the signs to integrate with the landscape. The signs mimic the trunks of the snow gums, aka eucalyptus trees. The system allows signs to be changed seasonally.

332

333

Index

30 St Mary Axe, 54
Aberrant decoding, 78
ADA, 122, 144
ADAAG, 122, 144
Advanced Technologies Centre, 42
Aicher, Otl, 110
Adidas Laces, 66
AIG Applied Information Group, 42, 160
AIGA, 106
Aiming, 40
Airport, 178, 182, 184, 186
ALT Group, 216
Analysing data, 170
Apps, 160
AR Augmented Reality, 165
Arbitrary SIGNS, 75
Ariadne, 28
Aristotle, 34
Arrows and more, 112
Ascender length, 99
Atletion, Aarhus, 48
Auckland Art Gallery, 216
Augmented Reality, 165
Avis, 124

Baker's pretzel, 78
Barlow, H.B, 34
Barthes, Roland, 58
bauer – konzept & gestaltung, 210
Berlin Brandenburg Airport, 178
Berra, Yogi, 32
Bikeway, Lisbon, 224
Braille, 151
Branding considerations, 174
Brisbane Airport, 182
British Library, 212
Brodsky, Joseph, 49
Budget Car, 124
Bureau Mijksenaar, 186, 218
Büro North, 228
büro uebele, 198, 214
Business-as-usual, 36, 53

Canterbury Shaker Village, 60, 94
Cases in point, 177
Centre Pompidou, 10, 144
Charles de Gaulle airport, 109
Chermayeff & Geismar, 36
Chinatown, 104
Chinese Wall, the, 62
Choice point, 135
Chrysler Building, 10
Clearview (typeface), 102
Cognitive maps, 24
Colour blindness, 149
Colour coding, 125
Colour, 119, 150
Commercial signs, 87
Compassing, 44
Comprehensibility, 80
Control Group, 192
Convention, 75
Crowdsourcing, 46

Decision, 19
Defining the problem, 169
Descender length, 99
Description, 60, 87, 94
Designations, 77
Designing graphics, 172
Designing hardware, 172
Developing a wayfinding strategy, 171
Diagrams, 76
Digital friend, a, 157
DIN Mittelschrift, 101
Direct aiming, 40
Direct labels, 53
Direction, 87, 92
Directional signs, 60
Distance, 94
Districts, 24
Doing without, 8

Eco, Umberto, 78
Edges, 24
Educated seeking, 34
Effectiveness level, 80
Eiffel Tower, 10, 54
Elephant Gate, 12
Emery Studio, 200, 226
Empire of Signs, 58
Empire State Building, 10
Environment, 53, 150
Ephesus, Turkey, 112
ERCO pictograms, 110
Escape route signs, 96, 112
Escaping a tsunami, 204
Eureka Parking, 200
Europcar, 124
Evaluating results, 173
Exclusive design, 147
Execution decision, 22
Explanation, 74, 87
Expo, 106
External information, 19

Falls Creek Alpine Resort, 228
Fifth Avenue, New York, 112
Flat mounted signs, 140
Floor-signs, 140, 141
Flyen, Bent, 194
Föhrenbusch, 12
Format, 128
Forward-up-alignment, 64
Forward-up-equivalence, 64
Four Seasons Restaurant, 87
Freestanding signs, 140
Frost Design, 182, 184, 208
Frutiger (typeface), 101
Fukuda, Shigeo, 106
Funicular, Bergen, 46

George Swinburne building, 74
Gherkin, the, 54
Global landscape architects, 202, 224
Gloriette, the, 53
Google Earth, 160

Google Maps, 160
GPS, 26
Graffiti, 15
Grids, 130
Grouping, 132
Guggenheim museums, 10
Guidelines, 117
Guiraud, Pierre, 74

Haakestad, Lise, 194
Hänsel und Gretel, 28
Head-up, 64
Heathrow airport, 68
Height, 138
Heinz, Mette, 68
Help desks, 6, 66
Help point, 66
Hertz, 124
Heuristics, 5
Historically enriched environment, 46
Hollywood sign, 55
Holmes Wood, 110, 212
Homing, 32
Hong Kong Metro, 20
HSBC, 78
Hyojitou, 190

IC tip, 190
Icons, 76
Identification, 90
IKEA, 28
Images, 76
Implementing the plan, 173
Inclusive vs. exclusive design, 147
Index 75, 77
Indication, 74
Indices, 75, 77
Indirect aiming, 40
Inference, 36
Info (typeface), 101
Initial planning, 21
Injunction, 74
Instruction, 74, 87
Intelligent seeking, 26
Interactive wayshowing, 156
Internal information, 19
ISO, 106

Jaenichen, Claudine, 204
JR Japan Railways, 6, 188, 190
JR Tokai Shinkansen, 188

Kew Gardens, 222
Kiosks, 159
Koyama, Keiichi, 125, 188

La Bibliotèque Nationale de France, 44
Landmarks, 24, 54
Learning from Las Vegas, 10
Legible London, 42
Legibility, 80, 99
L'Escargot, 90
Levels of communication, 73, 80

Lighting, 144
Line lengths, 100
Line spacing, 100
Location, 135
London Eye, 54
London underground, 28
Lorenz, Konrad, 81
Loss of vision, 149
Lufthansa, 76
Lumen, 144
Luna Park, 90
Lux, 144
Lynch, Kevin, 24

Macro method, 147
Make it Clear, 222
Make it Digital, 222
Makepeace Woodcraft School, 114
Map projection, 62
Map reading, 42
Map scale, 62
Map signatures, 62
Maps, 62
Maritime Museum Rotterdam, 218
Mayer / Reed, 196, 206
Means (vision), 150
Meeker & Associates, 102
Medici, 78
Melbourne Convention and Exhibition Centre, 66
Melbourne Park, 226
Mental map, 24
Mental model, 24
Mental solution, 22
Messages, 73, 74
Metaphors, 76
Metro, Copenhagen, 94
Metro, Washington DC, 30
Metropolitana Milanese, 62
Micro method, 147
Mies van der Rohe, 10
Mise èn scene, 134
Mixed strategies, 48
Moniteurs, 178
Moorfields Saddle, Victoria, 93
Motion, 19
Motivated SIGN, 75
Mounting, 140
Mount Rushmore, 55
MTA, New York, 192
Museum Moderner Kunst, Vienna, 84
MuseumsQuartier, Vienna, 84, 142

NCS Colour Circle, 120, 122
NCS Colour Space, 120, 122
NCS Colour Triangle, 120, 122
NCS Natural Colour System, 120
Need for planning, the, 167
No Way Through, 30
Nodes, 24
Non-commercial signs, 87
North up principle, 64
NSB Norwegian State Railways, 194

W>W 231

Index

Off-route information, 19
Olympic Games, 109, 110
On-route information, 19
On-route planning, 21
Oodnadatta, 16
Opera House, Sydney, 10
Optimising, 38
Orientation, 137
Oslo Airport, 132
Osnabrück University of Applied Science, 214

P-06 Atelier, 202, 220, 224
Parken Stadium, 37
Pasteur, Louis, 68
Paths, 24
Pawnbroker, 78
Penzias, Arno, 34
Persuasiveness, 80
Physical solution, 22
Piano, Renzo, 10
Pictograms, 106
Placeshowing, 20
Planar maps, 24
Planning, 166
Planning and execution, 21
Planning decision, 22
Planning process, the, 168
Planning signage, 171
Portable maps, 62
Practical theory, 72
Practicalities, 154
Practices, 176
Pre-visit information, 68
Progressive disclosure, 135
Problem solving process, 19
Projection, 62
Protruding signs, 140
Psychological tunnels, 29

Qantas check-in, 184
QR codes, 164, 190

Rails, 188, 190, 192, 194
RAL, 122
Random seeking, 26
Rauchfangkehrer, 54
Readability, 99
Reagents, 77
Redundancy, 70
Regulation, 60, 87, 96
Representation, 74
RFID, 190
Road detour, 28
Road signs, 81
Rogers, Richard, 10
Route following, 30
Royal Botanic Gardens, Kew, 222
Royal Botanic Gardens, Sydney, 93
Rule-following, 26
Russell Square, London, 112

Sadolin, Ebbe, 46

Santa Barbara, 204, 114
Satisficing, 38
Scale, 62
Schönbrunn, 53
Screening, 38
Seagram Building, 87
Search, 19
Seeking information, 170
Self-explanation, 53
Semantic level, 80
Semiology, 74
Sense-making, 26
Serendipity, 49
Setting the team, 169
Shannon, Claude E., 80
Sign categories, 87
Sign contents, 98
Sign form, 118
Sign functions, 86
Sign location and readability, 137
Signa (typeface), 101
Signage without signs, 9
Signatures, 62
Signification, 73, 75
Signified, 75
Signifier, 75
Signposting for visually impaired users, 146
Signs, 60
Simon, Herbert, 14, 38
Simplicity vs. redundancy, 70
Size, 127
Smartphone apps, 26, 160
Social navigation, 46
Social signifiers, 46
Solvitur ambulando, 22
Space economy, 99
State Library of New South Wales, the, 208
St. Olavs Hospital, 126, 130, 149
St. Stephansdom, 127
Steinberg, Saul, 24
Strip-map, 24
Suspended signs, 140
Swedish airports, 132
Syllogism, 34
Symbols, 75, 78

Tactile letters, 152
Tactile maps, 152
Tail of the Pup, 10
TAP – Théâtre et Auditorium Poitiers, 220
Targeting, 38
Technical level, 80
Terminology, 5
The Image of the City, 24
The Mathematical Theory of Communication, 80
The New Yorker, 25
Theory of SIGNS, 73
Tibirke, Denmark, 114
Toponomy, 56
Track following, 28
Trade Fair Stuttgart, 198
Trailblazing, 51

TriMet Portland Transit Mall, 196
Trump Tower, 84
Type size, 100
Typography, 99

Univers (typeface), 101
UPC, 164
Upper Austrian Federal State Library, Linz, 210
User instructions, 9
User interface 20

Vancouver Community Library, 206
Vandringer i Venedig, 46
Venturi, Brown, Izenour, 10
Vertical signs, 102, 104
Vienna, 114
Virgin Atlantic, 110
Visual impairment, 149
Visual user interface, 9
Vox populi, 14

Walk Brighton 161
Warning signs, 96
Washington Dulles International Airport, 186
Water Formula, 202
Wayfinder characteristics, 137
Wayfinding, 18
Wayfinding process, 22
Wayfinding strategies, 26
Waylosing, 49
Wayshowing, 50
Wayshowing hierarchy, 53
Wayshowing problems, 20
Weaver, Warren, 80
Why signs don't work, 73, 82
WWW, 158

You-are-here maps, 42, 62, 64

Sources

1000 Signs. (2004).
Cologne: Taschen.

Aicher, O. & Krampen, M. (1977).
Zeichensysteme der visuellen Kommunikation.
Stuttgart: Alexander Koch.

Americans with Disabilities Act. (1993).
The White Paper (2nd ed.).
Cambridge, Massachusetts: SEGD.

Arthur, P. & Passini, R. (1992).
Wayfinding: People, Signs, and Architecture.
Whitby: McGraw-Hill Ryerson.

Baines, P. & Dixon, C. (2003).
Signs: lettering in the environment.
London: Laurence King Publishing.

Barker, P. and Fraser, J. (no year).
Sign Design Guide.
London: JMU and the Sign Design Society.

Barthes, R. (1982).
Empire of Signs.
New York: Hill & Wang.

Bauer, E. K. & Mayer, D. (2009).
Orientation & Identity: Portraits of International Way Finding Systems.
Vienna: Springer.

Berger, C. M. (2005).
Wayfinding: Designing and Implementing Graphic Navigational Systems.
Mies, Switzerland: RotoVision.

Bertin, J. (1983).
Semiology of Graphics.
Madison, Wisconsin: The University of Wisconsin Press.

Bringhurst, R. (1999).
The Elements of Typographic Style.
Point Roberts, Washington: Hartley & Marks.

Brodsky, J. (1993).
Watermark.
New York: Farrar, Straus and Giroux.

Brown, J. S. & Druguid P. (2000).
The Social Life of Information.
Boston: Harvard Business School Press.

Bygg ikapp Handikapp. (2001).
Stockholm: Svensk Byggtjänst.

Carpman, J. R. & Grant, M. A. (1993).
Design That Cares.
San Francisco: Joissey-Bass.

Cité Internationale Universitaire de Paris: Integral Ruedi Baur et Associés. (2004).
Paris: Jean Michel Place.

Colour Atlas 96. (Ed. 3). (1996).
Stockholm: Swedish Standard SS 02 91 02.

Covington, G. A. & Hannah, B. (1997).
Access by Design.
New York: Van Nostrand Reinhold.

Crossby, Fletcher, Forbes. (1970).
A Sign System Manual.
London: Studio Vista.

Designprogrammet for OOL. (1994).
Oslo: Kulturdepartementet & Norsk Form.

Dreyfuss, H. (1972).
Symbol Sourcebook.
New York: McGraw-Hill.

Dutch Sign Design. (1995).
Amsterdam: BIS Publishers.

Expo 02 La Signalétique: Integral Ruedi Baur et Associés. (2002).
Paris: Jean Michel Place.

Fawcett-Tang, R. (Ed.). (2002).
Mapping.
Mies, Switzerland: RotoVision.

Garland, K. (1994).
Mr. Beck's Underground Map.
Harrow Weald UK: Capital Transport Publishing.

Golledge, Reginald G. (Ed.). (1999).
Wayfinding Behaviour.
Baltimore: John Hopkins University Press.

Grafiske tegn. (1987).
Piktogrammer til information af offentligheden
Del 1: Forbud, anvisninger m.m.
Copenhagen: Dansk Standard.

Guiraud, P. (1975).
Semiology.
London: Routledge.

Hellmark, C. (1998).
Underjordiska bokstäver.
Stockholm: Biblis 1 98.

Herdeg, W. (Ed.).(1978).
Archigraphia.
Zurich: The Graphis Press.

Holland, DK. (1997).
Design in depth.
Rockport: Rockport.

Horwitz, R. P. (1985).
The Strip: An American Place.
Lincoln: University of Nebraska Press.

Huth, J. E. (2013).
The Lost Art of Finding Our Way.
Cambridge: The Belknap Press of Harvard University.

Identité visuelle de Centre Pompidou: Integral Ruedi Baur et Associés. (2001).
Paris: Jean Michel Place Editions.

Information Design Source Book. (2005).
IID Institute for Information Design Japan
Basel: Birkhäuser.

Integral Ruedi Baur. (2001).
Baden, Switzerland: Lars Müller Publishers.

Integral Ruedi Baur et Associés. (2004).
Paris: Pyramid.

Jacobson, R. (Ed.). (1999).
Information Design.
Cambridge, Massachusetts: The MIT Press.

Kern, H. (2000).
Through the Labyrinth.
Munich: Prestel.

Kneebone, P. (1980).
Signalétique.
Paris: Centre National de Documentation Pédagogique.

Köln Bonn Airport. (2003).
Paris: Jean Michel Place.

Left, Right, Up, Down: New Directions in Signage and Wayfinding. (2010).
Berlin: Gestalten.

Lloyd, P. B. & Ovenden, M. (2012).
Vignelli Transit Maps.
Rochester: RIT Cary Graphic Arts Press.

Lunger, C. & Scheiber, M. (2009).
Orientierung auf Reisen: Touristische Leitsysteme.
Berlin: DOM Publishers.

Lynch, K. (1960).
The Image of the City.
Cambridge, Massachusetts: MIT Press.

March, J. G. (1994).
A Primer of Decision Making.
New York: Free Press.

MetaDesign. (1999).
London: Thames & Hudson.

Meuser, P. & Pogade, D. (2010).
Construction and Design Manual: Wayfinding and Signage.
Berlin: DOM Publishers.

Miller, C. & Lewis, D. / Information Design Unit. (1999).
Wayfinding: Effective wayfinding and signing systems. Guidance for healthcare facilities. NHS Estates.
Norwich: Her Majesty's Stationery Office.

Mollerup, P. (1997).
Vägvisning i ett nytt gammaldags bibliotek.
In *Tidernas bibliotek.*
Stockholm: Statens Kulturråd.

Mollerup, P. (2005).
*Wayshowing:
A Guide to Environmental Signage.*
Baden, Switzerland: Lars Müller Publishers.

Monmonier, M. (1996).
How to lie with maps.
Chicago: The University of Chicago Press.

Morne, R. (1998).
Neon & Ljusskyltar.
Stockholm: Svensk Byggtjänst.

Müller-Brockmann, J. (1996).
Grid Systems.
Heiden, Switzerland: Verlag Niggli.

Naegele, I.& Baur, R. (2004).
Scents of the City.
Baden, Switzwerland: Lars Müller Publishers.

NCS Lightness table. (1998).
Stockholm: Scandinavian Colour Institute.

Nilson, K. G. (2004).
KG Nilsons Färglära.
Stockholm: Carlssons.

Norman, Donald A. (1988).
The Psychology of Everyday Things.
New York: Basic Books.

Nørhald, S. (1993).
Byens skilte.
Copenhagen: Kunstakademiets Forlag, Arkitektskolen.

Pennick, N. (1990).
Mazes and Labyrinths.
London: Robert Hale.

Powel, K. (1992).
Stansted: Norman Foster and the architecture of flight.
London: Fourth Estate.

Sources

Reisens estetikk: Norge langs veien, Håndbok 99. (1999).
Oslo: Norsk Form.

Rouard-Snowman. (1992).
Museum Graphics.
London: Thames & Hudson.

Sadolin, E. (no year).
Vandringer i Venedig.
Copenhagen: Carit Andersen.

Shannon, C. E. & Weaver, W. (1949).
The Mathematical Theory of Communication.
Urbana: The Illinois University Press.

Sign Design. (1986).
New York: PBC.

Simon, H. A. (1996).
The Sciences of the Artificial.
Cambridge, Massachusetts: MIT Press.

Smitshuijzen, E. (2007).
Signage Design Manual.
Baden, Switzerland: Lars Müller Publishers.

Spiekermann, E. & Ginger, E. M. (1993).
Stop Stealing Sheep & find out how type works.
Mountain View: Adobe Press.

Symbol signs: The development of passenger/pedestrian oriented symbols for use in transport-related facilities. (1993).
New York: The American Institute of Graphic Arts.

Symbol Signs. (1993).
New York: The American Institute of Graphic Arts.

Système(s) d'orientation pour la ville et son agglommération de Lyon. Intégral Ruedi Baur et Associés. (2001).
Paris: Jean-Michel Place Éditions.

This Way Please: Environmental Graphic Design Worldwide. (2009).
Singapore: Page One Publishing.

Thrift, J. (2005).
The designer and the grid.
Mies, Switzerland: RotoVision.

Tilgængelighed i detaljen. (2004).
Copenhagen: Landsforeningen af blinde og svagsynede

Topalian, A. (1980).
The Management of Design Projects.
London: Associated Business Press.

Trulove, J. G. (2000).
This Way.
Rockport: Rockport.

Wildbur, P. (1988).
Information Graphics.
London: Trefoil Publications.

Wildbur, P. & Burke, M. (1998).
Information Graphics.
London: Thames & Hudson.

Wurman, R. S. (2000).
Information Anxiety 2.
Indianapolis: Que.

Wurman, R. S. (1996).
Information Architects.
Zurich: Graphis Press Corp.

Yukio, O. (1987).
Pictogram Design.
Tokyo: Kashiwashobo.

Photo credits

Alt
300, 301, 302, 303

Bauer
291, 292, 293, 294

Bureau Mijksenaar
242, 243, 244, 304, 305, 306

Büro North
331, 332, 333

büro uebele
67, 223, 224, 267, 268, 269, 297, 298, 299

Control Group
65, 203, 252, 253, 254, 255

Emery Studio
270, 272, 272, 273, 326, 327, 328, 329, 330

Flöche, Jacob
154

Flyen, Bent
256, 257, 258, 259

Frost Design
231, 232, 233, 234, 235, 236, 237, 238, 239, 240, 241, 287, 288, 289, 290

Haig, Andrew
163

Holmes Wood
295, 296

Koyama, Keiichi
1, 246

Janichen, Claudine
280, 281

Kuys, Blair
18, 97

Mayer / Reed
262, 263, 264, 265, 266, 284, 285, 286

McGovern, Nick
28, 40, 64, 66

Meeker & Associates
109, 110, 111, 112

Mollerup, Per
2, 3, 4, 5, 6, 7, 8, 9, 10, 11, 12, 17, 19, 21, 22, 23, 24, 27, 29, 30, 31, 32, 33, 34, 35, 36, 37, 38, 39, 43, 44, 46, 47, 48, 49, 50, 51, 52, 53, 54, 56, 57, 58, 59, 61, 62, 73, 76, 77, 78, 79, 82, 83, 84, 85, 86, 87, 88, 90, 91, 92, 93, 94, 95, 96. 98, 99, 100, 101, 103, 104, 105, 113, 114, 115, 116, 117, 118, 119, 120, 121, 122, 123, 124, 125, 147, 148, 151, 152, 153, 155, 156, 157, 158, 159, 161, 165, 171, 172, 173, 174, 177, 188, 189, 190, 191, 192, 193, 194, 195, 216, 217, 222

Moniteurs
225, 226, 227, 227

Muratovski, Gjoko
162, 164

Ozcan, A CanCan
147

Pacheco, Antonio
221, 315, 316

P-06 Atelier
274, 275, 276, 277, 278, 307, 308, 309, 310, 320, 321, 322, 323

Taffe, Simone
13, 14, 15, 16

Acknowledgements

This book would not have materialised without help from friends and colleagues.

At Swinburne University of Technology, Melbourne, Distinguished University Professor Ken Friedman polished the language and offered valuable editorial advice.
Dr. Simone Taffe, Dr. Blair Kuiff, Dr. Gjoko Muratovsky, and PhD Candidate Andrew Haig contributed with photos from several countries.
Dr. Kathrine Hepworth contributed with graphic design assistance and proof reading.
Design students Katelyn Testa and Nick McGovern contributed with graphic design assistance.

Designers Nina Kampmann and Bastian Andersen contributed with graphic design assistance.
Designer Antonio Pacheco contributed with photos.

Thanks.

Per Mollerup

Per Mollerup, Dr.Tech., MBA, has since 2009 been Professor of Communication Design at Swinburne University of Technology, Faculty of Design, Melbourne.

From 2007 to 2010 Per Mollerup served as Professor of Design at The Oslo National Academy of the Arts in Norway.

From 1984 to 2009, Per Mollerup was the owner and principal of Designlab in Copenhagen, an award-winning Danish design consultancy specialised in wayshowing and branding. Clients included airports, transportation companies, hospitals, museums, and private companies.

www.permollerup.com

Other books by Per Mollerup include:

Data Design
Visualising quantities, locations, connections (2013)
Bloomsbury Academic, London

Marks of Excellence
The History and Taxonomy of Trademarks (2013)
Phaidon, London
Revised and expanded edition of the 1997 edition

PowerNotes
Slide Presentations Reconsidered (2011)
Swinburne University of Technology, Melbourne /
IIID International Institute for Information Design, Vienna
Downloadable from
http:/hdl.handle.net/1959.3/191214

Brandbook
Branding, Feelings, Reason (2008)
Børsens Forlag, Copenhagen
In Danish

Collapsibles
A Design Album of Space-Saving Objects (2002)
Thames & Hudson, London